In the City of the D

In the City of the Marabouts

Islamic Culture in West Africa

Geert Mommersteeg
Utrecht University

Translated by
Diane Webb

WAVELAND

PRESS, INC.

Long Grove, Illinois

For information about this book, contact:
    Waveland Press, Inc.
    4180 IL Route 83, Suite 101
    Long Grove, IL 60047-9580
    (847) 634-0081
    info@waveland.com
    www.waveland.com

This book is the translation of *In de stad van de marabouts* (4th enlarged and revised edition, 2009). For the 2012 English-language edition by Waveland Press, the publisher and author gratefully acknowledge both the Netherlands Organization for Scientific Research (www.nwo.nl) and the Dutch Foundation for Literature (www.letterenfonds.nl) for their subsidy of the translation by Diane Webb.

Cover: Marabout transcribing a lesson for his pupil, Djenné, Mali. Photograph copyright © 2010 by David Sutherland. **Frontispiece:** Detail of Great Mosque, Djenné, Mali.

Chapter photographs (unless stated otherwise) are copyright © 1994, 1987 by Martin Stoop.

Printed in the United States of America

7   6   5   4   3   2   1

For Nan

Contents

Acknowledgments

*I*n Djenné, as elsewhere in West Africa, a conversation cannot really begin until each party has asked after the health and well-being of the other and his or her family, friends, and neighbors. Likewise this book cannot really begin until I have thanked all those who have contributed to it in some way. Given its long history, this involves a considerable number of people. Though I must confine myself here to mentioning only a few by name, I would like to emphasize my gratitude to each and every one of them.

This book is the translation of *In de stad van de marabouts* (4th enlarged and revised edition, 2009, Aksant Publishers, Amsterdam). That publication is based on my PhD thesis (Utrecht University, the Netherlands, May 1996), which contains the results of the anthropological research I carried out in Djenné in Mali. First of all, I would like to thank those who have assisted me from the very beginning, my professors and thesis supervisors Bonno Thoden van Velzen and Wouter van Beek.

My first two periods of fieldwork, which were also the longest (October 1985–October 1986 and June 1987–January 1988), were financed by the Netherlands Foundation for the Advancement of Tropical Research (WOTRO; grant W 52-368). Later visits to Djenné were made possible by Aramco World Services, the Dutch National Museum of Ethnology in Leiden, the Department of Cultural Anthropology at Utrecht University, and the Embassy of the Netherlands in Bamako, Mali. I am grateful to all of these organizations for their financial assistance. I also owe a debt of thanks to the Institute of Social Sciences, Bamako and the Malian administrative authorities, who gave me permission to carry out my research.

I am extremely grateful to the residents of Djenné—particularly the Kouroumansé family—who welcomed me warmly to their city, and of course all the marabouts who were kind enough to answer my questions and share their knowledge with me. The names of the marabouts who appear in this book have been changed for reasons of privacy.

Boubakar Kouroumansé's name is real, however. Boubakar's contribution as my research assistant and interpreter was of invaluable importance to my fieldwork. It is difficult to put into words how grateful I am for our long-standing collaboration and friendship. The "we" often used in this book gives sufficient emphasis, I hope, to the part he played in gathering fieldwork material. The use of the first person plural—for which the term *pluralis ethnographicus* might be coined—also underlines the fact that ethnographic knowledge must be considered a collective product.

I also want to express my appreciation for the support of Inez Fernig and the late Geert Zwart, and Dick Raateland, whose stay in Djenné as a member of the Dutch Volunteers (SNV) coincided in part with my stay and in whose houses—complete with shower and refrigerator—I was always welcome. I thank Pierre Maas, Rogier Bedaux, Annette Schmidt, and Phillippe Lemineur, with whom I have been privileged to work on a number of "Djenné projects" over the years, for their collaboration and friendship. I have received encouragement from a number of colleagues and friends. In particular, I want to express my gratitude for the support of Wil Pansters, Gerdien Steenbeek, Brenda Carina Oude Breuil, and Jan Jansen.

For the earlier editions of this book I am grateful to Prometheus Publishers (Amsterdam), Aksant Publishers (Amsterdam), Sjaak van der Geest, Éditions Grandvaux (Brinon-sur-Sauldre), Constant Hamès, Joseph Brunet-Jailly, and Mireille Cohendy, and particularly to my good friend Peter van Koningsbruggen, who read the first manuscript carefully and made valuable suggestions for improvements. I am indebted to Jan Peters, Ronald Kon, Louis Brenner, and Gerard van de Bruinhorst for their translations of various texts and terms in Arabic.

I am grateful to Tom Curtin for the wonderfully enthusiastic way in which he welcomed my book to Waveland Press and for the attention he has given to its production. The English edition would not have been possible without the support of the Netherlands Organization for Scientific Research (NWO) and the Dutch Foundation for Literature (DFL). My meticulous and skillful translator, Diane Webb, has proved herself to be a true wordsmith. I am grateful for the time she has lavished on my text and our enjoyable collaboration, which has allowed me to tackle this book again with pleasure. Finally, I thank Martin Stoop, friend and photographer, for his photos that enrich this book, especially the eight wonderful portraits of marabouts (from among the roughly fifty who contributed to my research) placed at the opening of each chapter. Inserted alphabetically, there is no direct correlation between the marabout portrayed and the subject matter of the chapter.

There remains but one acknowledgment, for which I refer the reader to the dedication at the front.

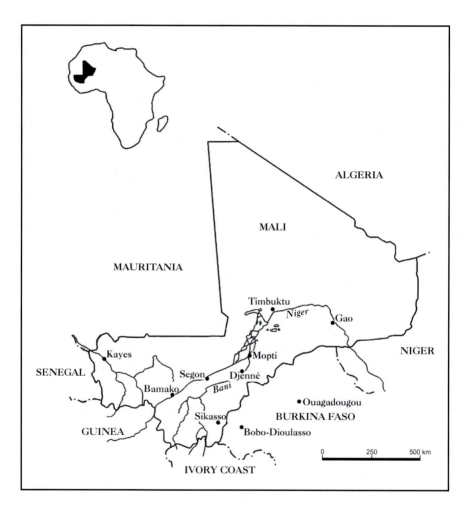

ALGERIA

MALI

MAURITANIA

Timbuktu
Niger
Gao

Kayes
NIGER

SENEGAL
Segon
Mopti

Bamako
Bani
Djenné

Ouagadougou
Sikasso
BURKINA FASO

GUINEA
Bobo-Dioulasso

0   250   500 km

IVORY COAST

Prologue

*M*ahaman, Boubakar's older brother, told me about an amulet he had that protected him whenever he took a trip anywhere. Every time he approached a police checkpoint he would push the leather armband containing the amulet higher up his arm and say to himself, "May God protect me from the police."

Once when Mahaman was traveling by *taxi-brousse* to Abidjan, all of the other passengers were searched at every checkpoint. Most of them were told that their papers were not in order, but after paying a fine, they were allowed to continue their journey. Mahaman was never asked to show his papers. One of his fellow passengers noticed this, and asked him why. Where did he come from, the man wanted to know. From Djenné, Mahaman replied. Oh, the man said, that explains everything. In Djenné, everyone is a marabout. It's the city of the marabouts.

He wasn't a marabout, Mahaman explained, and his father wasn't either. They were both masons. No, he was not a marabout. But he did have faith in God. That was all he needed.

Bamor Dembelé (ca. 1922–2004)

Chapter 1

Going Thirsty in Djenné

$\mathcal{S}$ome of the cracks in the mud ceiling looked like ancient rock drawings. Above my bed there seemed to be two running men, one holding a spear, the other a bow and arrow. That afternoon they trembled before my eyes. The stylized horse they were chasing had suddenly collapsed. I had a terrible headache, with a stabbing pain behind my eyes, which had begun late in the morning, about four hours earlier. At first it was a nagging ache, then came the stabs, lasting longer each time. My temples were throbbing, and my upset stomach was getting worse. I felt limp, but I could put up with that. Worst of all was the thirst. Shortly before sunrise I'd taken my last gulp of water—unthinkable in such heat. The hottest month of the hottest season in the Sahel had been at its hottest for several days now. It was necessary to drink three to four liters of water a day to make up for the moisture lost through perspiration. And now, for a full ten hours, not a drop. Just outside the door, on the veranda, stood a large earthenware jar, holding at least 40 liters of wonderfully cool water.

Boubakar's oldest sister, Nakeydya, had filled the jar the day before. Even though she would give birth to her seventh child any day now, she had gone twice to the communal tap outside the next row of houses and filled a large bucket with water. "Gérard, water," she cried from the courtyard below, before carrying the bucket upstairs on her head. Little Sekou followed his mother up the steps as usual, and peered shyly into the room, where I sat poring over my notes.

Luckily, I couldn't see the water jar from my bed, but how wonderful it would have tasted, how refreshing it would have been. Still, I couldn't give up now. After all, I wasn't ill, I was working—working hard, in fact, doing anthropological fieldwork in Islamic West Africa. I was doing participant-observation research, which entailed taking part in the fasting month of Ramadan.

Toward sunset the previous evening—May 9, 1986—many of those living in the old city of Djenné in Mali had stared at the cloudy western sky, waiting for the appearance of the thin crescent of the new moon that would announce the beginning of Ramadan—or *hawme* (literally, to tie the mouth), as the month of fasting is called in the Songhay language. No one had seen it, however, not even the men who had stayed after evening prayer to search for the moon from the raised platform on which Djenné's Great Mosque stands. Still, anyone who imagined he had caught a glimpse of the pale moon between the clouds would have thought twice before announcing it. A few years before, a man named Ko Kontao had supposedly sighted the new moon of Ramadan, but he was the only one in the city to make such a claim. A year later, people were still addressing him mockingly as Handu Ko Kontao (in Songhay, *handu* means both moon and month).

It was 10:00 PM before the residents of Djenné knew that Ramadan had actually begun. Only when Radio Mali announced that the moon had been sighted in Bougouni, in the south of the country, could they be certain that the following day would mark the beginning of their observance of the fourth pillar of Islam: for 29 or 30 days—depending on when the next new moon was sighted—one was supposed to abstain, from sunrise to sunset, from eating, drinking, smoking, and sexual intercourse. After the radio report, town criers walked through the streets, loudly proclaiming the beginning of hawme.

Fasting had been a favorite topic of conversation long before Ramadan officially began. To experience for myself what it meant to fast, I had promised—more or less on a whim—to observe the first day of Ramadan. Boubakar Kouroumansé, with whom I had been working for a couple of months, was delighted, but I was now beginning to regret my rash decision. In addition to my pounding head and dry throat, my back had started to protest: the straw mattress I was lying on was becoming more uncomfortable by the minute.

*S*ix months earlier: October 1985. A warm wind was blowing through the open window of the taxi that was taking me from the airport to the center of the capital city of Bamako. Fearing I might fall out, I edged away from the rusty door, which was held together by wire, and also tried not to put my weight on my feet, since I could see the road flashing past through the holes in the floor of the car. The taxi driver was not very talkative. The sticker on the windshield said "Dieu Merci" in the midst of Arabic letters. I, too, thanked God for watching over this rattling, patched-up old car.

Africa glided past. After a few kilometers the landscape began to show signs of habitation. Red mud houses—some in a state of dilapidation and others under construction—shops with painted signs above their entrances, warehouses with heavy iron shutters and doors: these buildings formed a more or less continuous row some distance away. Nearer to the road were food stands and little shops made of corrugated iron. We passed taxi-buses packed with people, and pickup trucks with passengers squeezed together in the back. Bicycles, mopeds, and pedestrians were urged to the side of the road by honking vehicles. Everywhere there were people with baskets or bowls on their heads, bicycle and moped racks laden with boxes, packages, and bulky sacks, and car roofs piled high with goods—nearly everyone was transporting a load of some kind.

We crossed the bridge over the Niger and ended up in the heavy traffic of Bamako. Noise and exhaust fumes filled the air as we neared the downtown area. The thick leaves of the trees in the gardens of big concrete bank buildings were covered with a thin layer of red dust. Some beggars were sitting in front of a pharmacy next to a fancy supermarket, waiting for customers to emerge. A taxi stand full of cars and people was bordered by a row of tables, behind which a number of women were stirring food in large pans on a wood fire. Two old, wrinkled posters on the peeling wall of the movie theater next door announced the program: an Indian love story and *Rocky III*. The taxi turned left. The road to the boardinghouse run by Catholic nuns was filled with huge potholes. The Spanish sister who managed the Centre d'Accueil Catholique let me in, gave me a mosquito net, and showed me to my bed.

Lying on my back with my hands behind my head, I stared at the whirring blades of two large ceiling fans. They brought little relief. I could hear the cars rattling past, their drivers often unable to avoid the potholes. Traffic, voices, shouts, music blaring from the cassette recorder of the boys below the open window: the outside noises rushed in through the blinds and took possession of the dormitory.

The shrill voice of a Malian singer stopped abruptly and was replaced by "We Are the World." Distorted by the high volume, this well-known number (six months earlier it had been the signature tune of the international relief drive for Africa's famine victims) now drowned out the street noise. "We are the world. We are the children. So let's start giving." The next number the boys played was again an African song.

It was too warm to eat much of anything. My lunch consisted of a cup of tea and a croissant at a sidewalk café in the middle of town. As soon as the Lebanese proprietress had brought my order, the parade began. Street vendors with trays of cassettes, cigarettes, toothpaste, and soap started to file past my table. Boys beat their brushes against their shoeshine boxes. An old woman stuck out a hand with fingers disfigured by leprosy. Young girls walked by, pointing to the platters of bananas and oranges balanced on their heads. A man crept up to the sidewalk tables like a spider. With his hands wrapped around his ankles, he pushed his wasted legs forward, dragging his buttocks along the ground. A blind singer in a long, once-white robe sang plaintively, his hand resting on the scrawny shoulder of a shabbily dressed boy holding a tin begging bowl. No sooner had the blind man finished his song than another boy with cassettes came past. "This one is especially good, sir," he said as he waved the cover in my face. "We Are the World," I read.

In the evening I wiled away the time talking to some of the other guests at the Centre d'Accueil. A German man told me that he had crossed the Sahara on a motorcycle and was planning to go back the same way. An American couple—Jean-Louis Bourgeois, an architectural historian, and Carolee Pelos, a photographer—invited me to eat with them in town. Dysentery had forced them to interrupt their tour of West Africa. The cure, they said, was worse than the disease. They both looked very emaciated. Over dinner they told me about their travels. They knew Djenné well. Obviously enthusiastic about its mud-brick buildings, they promised to show me the book they had written about adobe architecture, which included photos of Djenné's Great Mosque. The city was very beautiful, they said. When I told them about my research plans, they warned me that getting inside Djenné's rather closed society would not be easy.

I had been told the same thing by the American anthropologist Adria LaViolette, who had previously carried out research in the city. Djenné, she told me in a letter, would require patience. It would take time to win people's confidence and secure their cooperation. Those who had already collaborated with researchers from the West were beginning to tire of it. Others, she warned, clearly wanted nothing to do with white people.

I had received a research grant from the Netherlands Organization for Scientific Research to continue the work begun by other researchers. Since the early 1970s, archaeologists, anthropologists, anthropobiologists, social geographers, and architects—mostly from Dutch and American universities—had been investigating Djenné and its inhabitants. My aim was to add to that body of knowledge by doing anthropological research into the power structure of the city. The recent shifts in power relations were especially interesting. I planned to examine the role played by three groups in particular: artisans, traders, and religious specialists. Others had already gathered quite a bit of material on the artisans and traders, but far less was known about the marabouts, the Islamic scholars. Since they interested me the most, I planned to focus on them first.

At that time it was impossible to foresee that the world of the marabouts would claim all my attention and end up determining the course of my research. Anthropological fieldwork does not always go as planned; indeed, it often has its own dynamism.

In Bamako I became acquainted with Geert and Inez Zwart, two Dutch volunteers working on a public health project in a village in the Inland Delta of the Niger. They offered to take me to Djenné, but their car was in a garage, undergoing repairs. In the meantime, I set out to obtain the necessary visa and research permit. Day after day the mechanic swore that he was almost done with the car, but these endless delays proved to be convenient. I spent several mornings going from one government office to the next, calling at departments where the secretaries had fallen asleep over their typewriters, or the person in charge had just left, and his deputy was not allowed to sign official documents. Refusing to let this discourage me, I redoubled my efforts to obtain the right papers with the requisite signatures and endorsements, as well as the compulsory tax stamps.

*A*t last we could leave. Djenné was a day's journey from the capital: 700 kilometers of asphalt road, first northeast to Segou, then southeast to Bla, and again, via San, northeast until the turnoff to Djenné. The greatest change in the landscape occurred during the last 100 kilometers, from San on. It became less green and more open, drier and more expansive. Tall, thick baobab trees were scattered across the savannah. Termite hills of red earth, shaped like miniature cathedrals, towered two meters above the low brushwood. Gray mud houses and granaries stood out against the blue sky. Women and girls were washing clothes in a small lake at the edge of a village. The children who noticed us waved or came running toward the road. It was market day in one of the larger villages along the way. Buyers and sellers crowded around stalls made of wooden stakes covered with reed matting or sometimes a piece of plastic or canvas. An old truck was being loaded with sacks and baskets. Just outside the market, unharnessed mules were tethered next to the carts they would have to pull home at the end of the day. A few kilometers further on, a goat suddenly crossed the road. Inez slammed on the brakes as the rest of the flock appeared at the roadside. A young goatherd prodded the animals with his stick, urging them on.

A small concrete marker announced "Djenné," accompanied by a helpful arrow curving to the left. Leaving the black ribbon of asphalt behind us, we drove into the landscape. A 30-kilometer-long road, consisting mostly of a low dike, ran westward into the flood plains of the

Bani, a tributary of the Niger. Owing to a long stop at Segou, we had arrived at this point much later than planned. Darkness was already falling. The surface of the laterite road leading to the embankment had the ribbed texture of a washboard. Geert told me that you had to maintain a constant speed of 70 kilometers an hour, as anything else would make our Toyota Land Cruiser shake dreadfully. Later on I would travel this road in various African taxis-brousse; sometimes the driver had to stop his overcrowded vehicle in the middle of the dike, get out, and use his fist to pound the windshield back into place.

The branches of the trees on either side of the narrow road almost touched overhead, forming a tunnel. A few barren-looking fields were vaguely discernible in the darkening plain. By the time we reached the banks of the Bani, it was pitch dark and stars were twinkling in a moonless sky. The ferry that was supposed to take us across the river was tied up on the opposite shore. Officially, there was no ferry service after sunset, but our honks and shouts were answered by people who went to fetch the boatmen. In another four months, the broad river lying before us would be a mere stream that cars could easily ford. Now, however, we had no choice but to wait for the ferry. Geert and Inez said it might take a while.

At last we saw something drifting toward us: a rickety construction made of welded steel floats and planking, which barely rose above the surface of the water. It was propelled by several men with long bamboo poles. The dark figures of the boatmen were swallowed up by the dusk of early evening. It was not until they shook our hands that we were able to make out their faces. The car was cautiously driven onto the ferry, which was then punted—sometimes rocking perilously—to the opposite shore. After driving up the sandy bank of the Bani, we still had another four kilometers of embankment road. The huge potholes in its mud surface had to be negotiated with care.

Then, quite suddenly, we were in Djenné. The sight of the city looming up from the landscape and crowned by the towers of the Great Mosque—which makes a daytime arrival so unforgettable—was now obliterated by darkness. But arriving at night had its own charms. The car's headlights glided over thick mud walls and housefronts, and lit up the robes of the people in the street. In the market square we saw the flickering flames of the kerosene lamps on the merchants' tables of wares and the glowing fires of the meat sellers. Inez pointed to the side of the square where the mosque was, but it was too dark to see the famous edifice.

*I*n the late nineteenth century, Félix Dubois had come to Djenné by boat. After the French had conquered Djenné in April 1893 and Timbuktu at the end of that year, *Le Figaro* dispatched this experienced reporter to the newly acquired territories. The serialized account of Dubois's journey on the Niger, stopping at such places as Bamako, Segou, Djenné, and finally Timbuktu, was published in book form in France in 1897 and instantly became a best seller. That same year it was published in English as *Timbuctoo the Mysterious* (1969[1897]). Not only was the book a perfect reflection of the optimism of colonial expansion, but it also satisfied the penchant for the exotic so common in those days. The chapters Dubois devoted to Djenné are particularly lyrical.

In the early autumn of 1894, Dubois left the Niger just below the village of Kouakourou and traveled up one of its tributaries. According to his account, approximately 12 hours after leaving the great river the Bozo boatmen, who were making this journey for the first time, suddenly stopped punting the boat and stood, speechless, dangling their long bamboo poles. From beneath his reed-covered shelter, Dubois urged them on, but the men turned to him and pointed with amazement at what lay before them. In barely audible voices trembling with emotion, they stammered, "Djenné!"

His curiosity roused, Dubois went to the front of the boat, and he too was dumbstruck: "For the first time in these regions I was astounded by the work of man. There had been no shortage of curious and beautiful sights on my journey, but to the eye and mind of a cultivated man there was always something lacking, some trace of civilization to evoke the genius of humanity." Suddenly, however, Dubois was confronted with Djenné. And just as this Frenchman thought that such "precious gems" as Amboise, Tours, and Chambord made the Loire Valley a sight to behold, so he considered Djenné "the jewel of the Niger Valley."

Djenné was an enigma. How had this gem ended up here, "in the midst of a barbarous country"? The first thing Dubois did in his travel account, even before describing the city, was to delve into its origins. Dubois, who had previously traveled around the Near East, had an unusual theory. Even though the "jewel" of Djenné was situated in the Niger Valley, its origins lay in another river basin, namely that of the Lower Nile. For what else could possibly explain his feelings upon landing? Once inside the city walls, he immediately saw that this was not just one of those "disorderly clusters of dwellings" but "a real town" with broad streets, two-story houses, and façades displaying an architectural style "that instantly arrests the eye." What other explanation was there, other than the assumption that "the beneficent influence of Egypt, mother of Western civilization, penetrated the heart of the negro country"? It was clear to Dubois that the Songhay, whom he mistook for the founders of Djenné, were the heirs of Egyptian civilization and had simply exchanged the banks of the Nile for those of the Niger. They had, in his opinion, migrated westward and founded Djenné around 765, as recorded in the local seventeenth-century chronicle *Tarikh al-Sudan.*

"Wholly speculative" was how Charles Monteil (1903) described the theory that the Songhay had come from Egypt and had built in Djenné houses similar to those in their native country. According to the colonial administrator who governed Djenné from 1900 to 1903, Dubois's story, at least on this point, was pure fiction. There was nothing to substantiate his claim.

In his extremely detailed monograph, which can be regarded as the first scientific study of the city, Monteil situates Djenné's history in the region of the Inland Delta of the Niger. The Bozo, a fishing people, lived in small settlements scattered across the fertile plains where the Niger and the Bani flow together, before splitting into countless streams and rivulets. Among the very first migrants, who were thought to have come to this area centuries ago, were a group of Nono traders. They had come from Dia in the west and settled in the Bozo village of Djoboro. It was this village that eventually grew into a city.

Rising up out of the flat landscape three kilometers southeast of present-day Djenné is a large mound, which the residents of Djenné call Djenné-djeno, meaning "ancient Djenné." In 1977 and 1981, the American archaeologists Roderick and Susan McIntosh (1980, 1982) examined this ancient settlement mound. The results of their excavations were spectacular: carbon dating of charcoal from the hearths of the old settlement proved that the site had been inhabited as early as the third century BC. It was shown that even before the ninth century, this small Iron Age settlement had blossomed into a prosperous city with a completely urban way of life. This sensational discovery—the ruins of the oldest city south of the Sahara—disproved the theory that the cities of West Africa had not developed until centuries after Arabian traders from North Africa had traversed the Sahara to gain control of the trading routes. Urbanization, it turned out, had not taken place in the thirteenth century—as adherents of that theory maintained—but hundreds of years earlier.

In its heyday, ancient Djenné and its satellite settlements numbered some 20 thousand inhabitants. From around 1200 the population of the old city gradually dropped as people began to move to nearby Djenné. The reasons for the decline of Djenné-djeno are not clear, but the rise in Djenné of an elite group of Muslim traders was probably a decisive factor. The new aristocracy distanced itself from the polytheistic practices of the old city, the trading power of the traditional merchants waned, and the prosperity enjoyed by Djenné-djeno came to an end. In the mid-fifteenth century, the city was abandoned and left to decay. Erosion took its toll, until the oldest city in West Africa was absorbed into the landscape, while its Islamic offspring thrived.

According to the account given by the seventeenth-century historian Abderrahman al-Sadi in the *Tarikh al-Sudan*, at the end of the sixth century of the Hijra—around 1200 CE—4,200 Islamic scholars from the region gathered together in Djenné. They had been ordered by the ruler Koy Konboro to come to the city to witness his conversion to Islam. It is now generally assumed that al-Sadi's estimate was on the high side. Not only did he record the event some four and a half centuries after it happened, but he is unlikely to have been entirely objective, since he had been a long-time resident of Djenné, as well as an imam. Yet even if the numbers were less impressive than claimed, the presence of Islamic scholars in thirteenth-century Djenné illustrates that Islam had been spreading for some time in the regions to the south of the Sahara. First of all, starting in the eighth or ninth century, North African traders plying the caravan routes brought the new religion with them. Later on, in the eleventh century, the Almoravides—soldier-monks who came from the western Sahara—exerted their influence.

Regardless of how many Islamic scholars actually attended Konboro's conversion, the role they played in this event, which was so important to the history of Djenné, was not insignificant. Al-Sadi relates how Konboro renounced heathenism—an act he emphasized by tearing down his palace and putting up a mosque in its place—and ordered the assembled scholars to pray to God to grant Djenné three things: first, that all those who came to Djenné to escape the misery and poverty in their own countries would find such abundance that they would forget their homelands; second, that the city would be peopled by foreigners more numerous than the local population; and third, that all those who came to do business in Djenné would be robbed of their patience, so that they would grow weary of the place and sell their wares cheaply, to the benefit of the residents.

It was clear to al-Sadi that God had heard the scholars' supplications. All those gazing upon the prosperous city of Djenné in the mid-seventeenth century could see with their own eyes that Djenné was "large, thriving, and rich, and privileged by the Almighty who had bestowed on it all favors." Indeed, it had become "one of the leading mercantile centers of the Islamic world."

Even so, by the time of al-Sadi, the great West African empires were past their peak. The kingdom of Mali had disintegrated by the end of the fourteenth century, and the Songhay, who had captured Djenné in 1473, had been defeated in the last decade of the sixteenth century by a Moroccan expeditionary force. Particularly under the leadership of the great Songhay ruler Askia Mohammed (who reigned from 1493 to 1528) and his successors, trade and Islamic culture flourished as never before. Islamic teachers and their pupils enjoyed the dignitaries' hospitality and shared in the wealth that had been amassed in the urban commercial centers. The transportation routes over land and river came together in Djenné, a trading hub where salt, jewels, and textiles from the north were exchanged for gold, cola nuts, ivory, and slaves from the south. According to al-Sadi, sixteenth-century Djenné had 60 Qur'anic schools attended by 12,000 pupils. Again, even though this number should be taken with a grain of salt, it is indicative of the city's status as a center of Islam.

After the Songhay, things gradually went downhill. There was widespread discord in the Moroccan protectorate, and its rulers wielded little authority. Anarchy and chaos prevailed. The peaceful conditions that had allowed long-distance trade to flourish and had benefited the Islamic scholars and religious advocates no longer existed. Nevertheless, the Moroccans, or their offspring from mixed marriages, continued to occupy important positions in Djenné longer than elsewhere in the region. It was not until 1819 that a holy war put a definite end to more than two centuries of Moroccan rule. The reformer Seku Amadu, a Fulbe who had studied in Djenné in his younger years, declared a jihad. After he and his followers had captured the city, he founded a new capital—which he called Hamdallaye (from *al hamdu lillahi*, meaning praise to God)—on the right bank of the Bani, 60 kilometers northeast of Djenné. From here Seku Amadu ruled the conquered territories and governed his theocratic state. Even in Djenné, which was regarded as the regional center of Islam, he detected traditions that deviated from his orthodox notions. One particular thorn in his side was the great thirteenth-century mosque, which the Moroccans had defiled with what he considered sacrilegious practices. Upon his orders, the house of prayer was abandoned and left to deteriorate. In its stead Seku Amadu built a new—and much more austere—mosque.

As a result of the organization of the Fulbe empire, Djenné continued to decrease in importance as the political and religious capital of the Inland Delta of the Niger. René Caillié, who in 1828 became the first European to visit Djenné, remarked in his travel journal (1985[1830]) that when the pupils of the many Qur'anic schools in the city could learn no more, they were sent to Hamdallaye. In the 1860s, however, a new holy war put an end to the dominion of the Fulbe. They were replaced by the Tukulor, to whom they were related. Under the leadership of the conqueror Al-Hajj Umar Tall, the Tukulor succeeded—owing in part to the rifles they had obtained from European traders in exchange for slaves—in expanding their territory from Senegal further to the east. Their empire did not last long. Rivalry among Al-Hajj Umar Tall's successors made it

Djenné's weekly market, held in the square in front of the Great Mosque.

impossible to offer effective resistance to the advance of the French, which began around 1890.

In April 1893, Djenné was occupied by the troops of Colonel Louis Archinard. What had previously been a source of strength—its relative isolation in the flood plains of the Niger and Bani—led at the beginning of the twentieth century to further decline. The commercial activities that had made Djenné great had been taken over by Mopti, 100 kilometers to the north, which linked up more easily to the newly constructed roads. Under French influence Mopti developed into the regional capital.

In 1907 the colonial administrators opened the first *madrasah* in French West Africa. It was located in Djenné, the traditional center of Islamic education. One of the purposes of this school, at which instruction was given in both Arabic and French, was to instill in an elite group of young Muslims a correct view of the civilizing role played by the French in Africa. It proved impossible to recruit enough pupils, however, and in 1913 Djenné's madrasah closed its doors.

The other building that opened in Djenné in 1907 met with more success. On October 1 of that year the first prayer was held at the new mosque, whose construction had begun a year earlier on the remains of Konboro's first mosque in the center of the city. The townscape has been dominated ever since by the edifice that gradually became Djenné's trademark: its Great Mosque, which in 1988 was placed on UNESCO's World Heritage List.

Apart from the experiment with the madrasah, the French scarcely interfered with the religious domain in Djenné. Still, the city's glorious days as a center of Islamic education were definitely a thing of the past. Many young men went to work in the cities, which was certainly more lucrative than pursuing Islamic studies. The modern commercial center of Mopti gradually overshadowed the scholarly city of Djenné.

In 1960, when the Republic of Mali gained its independence, Djenné became the capital of the eponymous administrative *cercle*, which in turn was part of the *region* of Mopti. The growth of Mopti was ultimately responsible for the present-day character of Djenné, now a town of limited regional importance. Only the large weekly market, held every Monday in the square in front of the mosque, reflects the former glory of this trading town, where the ethnically diverse population—consisting of the Marka, Fulbe, Bozo, and, to a lesser extent, Rimaïbe, Bwa, Bamana, and several other small ethnic groups—numbered some 12 thousand souls in the second half of the 1980s.

Today, its isolation and limited economic importance mean that certain developments taking place elsewhere in Mali's Islamic community have largely passed Djenné by. For example, the reformist Wahhabi movement, whose origins and ideological roots lie in Saudi Arabia, has attracted growing numbers of followers, especially in such trading towns as Bamako, Segou, and Mopti. In the late 1980s, however, when I was doing my fieldwork in Djenné, its impact was still negligible.

*T*he first day of Ramadan began early. At 3:30 AM Boubakar came up to the roof of my house to wake me, so that we could eat before the sun came up. Beneath the nocturnal sky we walked through the dark streets to the house of Boubakar's family. In the courtyard where we ate together every evening was a bowl of rice with some sauce and a few chunks of fish. I had little appetite. Still half asleep, I scooped the rice into my mouth. After the meal, the family—clearly impressed by my good intentions—wished me good luck with my first day of fasting.

On the way back to my house we met several *garibus* (literally, strangers). These young Qur'anic pupils, who come to Djenné from villages in the surrounding area to study for longer or shorter periods, are forced to beg for their food. Having adapted their schedules to Ramadan, they now took to the streets with their begging gourds and tin cans in an attempt to collect their share of the last meal before the fasting began. "Friend of God, here is a stranger," we heard a couple of times in the stillness of the night.

On the veranda I lit the oil lamp and Boubakar lit a fire in the charcoal stove to boil water. We drank a cup of tea and talked about how difficult it would be. Boubakar had never fasted for a whole month, but he knew what it meant to go without food—and especially water—for an entire day. For a couple of years now the month of fasting had coincided with the hot season, and he had regularly fasted for a day with the others. Later, as a married man who no longer enjoyed the freedom of youth, he would be expected to fast for the entire month. He already knew that the first day was especially hard, but one fasted for God, and He did not always make things easy for the faithful.

Boubakar went to his room to sleep a while longer, and I returned to my mat on the roof. Between 5:15 and 5:30 AM, as the towers of the mud-brick mosque were becoming visible in the east, I picked up the flask I had next to me and took a last large gulp of water. I managed to sleep until 7:45, when the warm rays of the sun made it unpleasant to stay on the roof any longer. At 8:00 AM, the familiar voice of the newsreader on Radio Netherlands Worldwide could be heard on the veranda, where it was still rather cool. The tea and bread that I normally consumed along with the news were missing today. My first Ramadan had begun.

The first day of fasting also marked the beginning of the daily gatherings, held at various places in the city, at which marabouts read aloud from the Qur'an and the accompanying exegetical commentary (*tafsîr*). They would continue to do this throughout the month, reading each day one-thirtieth of the Holy Book and the relevant exegesis, as formulated by sixteenth-century Arabic scholars. Around 10:00 AM Boubakar came to fetch me to attend the gathering led by the marabout Alfa Baba Kampo. Until then I had been at my desk, trying to work on my notes, but it had not been a productive morning.

I took my Qur'an and we walked to the neighborhood where Kampo lived and kept a school at which various branches of Islamic studies were taught. To accommodate those attending the readings, a large canopy had been set up in the square near Kampo's house. About a hundred men, most of them elderly, sat on reed mats around the marabout. They were listening to his melodious reading of the Arabic text and its sing-song translation into Songhay. Some of the listeners had the Qur'an or the volume of exegesis open before them and were reading along in silence. A number of older women were following the proceedings from the doorways of their houses, which bordered on the square. Half-hidden behind the open doors, they sat there unobtrusively, almost invisible to the men. As they listened, they kept on with their work, sewing beads on bracelets. Now and then Boubakar pointed to a passage in my Qur'an, to the right-hand column with the Arabic text, to show me how far the reading had progressed. In the left-hand column I read the Dutch translation of God's Word.

When thirst threatened to overcome me in the stifling heat under the canopy, I forced myself to concentrate on the reading, sometimes observing the people around me. I understood nothing of what was read, but the rhythmic recitation had a pleasant sound. I reminded myself that the others were fasting as well. Kampo read without a break until 1:30 PM. When the reading was finished, a couple of men came over to us and asked with interest if they might be allowed to look at my Qur'an. The Arabic text convinced them: it was indeed the Holy Book.

*N*ext to my bed stood a chair made of curved branches strapped together with goat-leather laces. A book and my watch lay on this African version of the Thonet bentwood chair. Reading—otherwise a relaxing distraction during the midday rest period—was out of the question, because of the stabbing pain in my head. The watch was not of interest either; keeping track of the time would only make the hours go by more slowly. I dozed despite my headache and thirst. Until about 5:30 PM I stuck it out on the bed, then shakily climbed the narrow stairs to the roof, where I slumped, completely drained, in a chair. The sun was already in the west, though still quite a way above the horizon. I would have done anything to make it set.

Anthropologists are adventurous. They go to live in foreign places, eat strange food, try to speak foreign languages, and take part in customs unfamiliar to them. From close up and preferably from the inside, anthropologists observe and experience how others live their lives, how they organize their activities and bestow meaning on them. They want to get as close as possible to the daily lives of others. By participating in their activities, by asking questions and making firsthand observations, anthropologists seek to understand things that people in other societies consider meaningful and important. It is the application of this so-called participant-observation method that distinguishes anthropology from the other social sciences.

The success or failure of anthropological fieldwork depends on the kind of relationship fieldworkers manage to establish with the people in whose city, village, or group they temporarily reside. The important thing is the interaction, the rapport between researchers and their hosts. The recognition of the fundamentally human character of the undertaking is indispensable to its success.

The way in which I shared my human identity with the residents of Djenné on that first day of fasting manifested itself mainly in an empty stomach and a dry throat. A few years before, while doing research for my master's thesis in the clammy heat of Surinam's tropical forest, I had been plagued by visions of ice-cold beer and soft drinks. I swore then that if I ever undertook anthropological fieldwork again, it would be among the Lapps or the Inuit, in any case, somewhere near the polar circle. But here I was after all, suffering from thirst in the Sahel. Three hundred fifty kilometers to the north lay Timbuktu, the city to which Donald Duck flees whenever the going gets tough. How would a duck feel after a day out of water?

In handbooks on anthropological research, the first important field-work undertaken by a beginning anthropologist is sometimes compared with an initiation rite, such as the rituals that in traditional societies mark the transition from one phase of life to the next—in particular the passage from youth to adulthood. According to the French anthropologist Arnold van Gennep, who introduced the term *rites de passage* in 1909, such rites of passage always follow a set pattern, in which three phases can be distin-guished: the person in question undergoes separation, passes through a transitional period, and finally reenters society with a new status. It is argued that this three-phase model of the initiation ritual is also applica-ble to anthropological fieldwork. After all, anthropologists leave their own culture, isolate themselves in the field to become acquainted with a new culture, and then return to write up their results and produce a dis-sertation, thereby acquiring the status of professional anthropologist. In many rites of passage, the liminal phase of transition is accompanied by deprivation. Initiates are generally subjected to various kinds of hardship, and I realized that going thirsty in Djenné was a perfect example of a sec-ond-phase ordeal.

After sitting listlessly on the roof for just under an hour, I decided to go to the house of Boubakar's family. I usually enjoyed the sight of the mud city in the late afternoon light, when the low sun turned the walls a beauti-ful shade of orange and the houses contrasted stunningly with the length-ening shadows. Today, however, its beauty failed to move me. My only concern was my body, which moved slowly and craved water. How could anyone fast for a whole month in this climate? A number of people had assured me that it would become easier after four or five days, but I was not inclined to spend an unproductive month finding that out for myself.

There was not much life in the courtyard. Everyone was tired and sluggish, their faces clearly marked by an entire day of fasting. Voices that were otherwise lively sounded muffled. Hardly anyone spoke. The signal that we could drink again had not yet been given. At around 6:45 PM Fati-mata, the second wife of Boubakar's older brother Mahaman, rushed back from the tap in the square, where she had heard that the signal had

A street in the Yoboukayna quarter on the west side of Djenné.

been given at the mosque: the first day of fasting was officially over. Water, water!

Boubakar's father made the rounds with a bowl containing a whitish liquid. *Baani hari* (soft water) was what they called the curdled milk mixed with sugar and water. The luxurious ice cubes floating in it, which had been fetched from a vendor with a kerosene refrigerator, underlined the significance of the occasion: the first breaking of the fast. Everyone drank the icy cold liquid. It tasted wonderful, and so did the date we ate with it.

That evening I ate very little. A few millet cakes and a couple of handfuls of rice were all I could manage. I washed it down with huge gulps of water. My first day of fasting was over.

That month I would submit once again to the rigors of fasting: on the twenty-seventh day of Ramadan—the day following the *Laylat al-Qadr*, the Night of Power, which is the anniversary of the night in which the Qur'an says it was revealed—when keeping the fast is considered especially praiseworthy. That day, too, I spent most of the afternoon lying lethargically on my bed.

Two days out of 30. I admit it was not very many, and even though one or two of the younger men continued to tease me by calling me *jaari hinka* (two days) whenever they saw me, those two days had not been completely unproductive. On various occasions people told me how much they appreciated my willingness to fast, even for that short amount of time. Moreover, my frequent presence at the tafsîr readings did not go unnoticed. During the month of fasting, news spread of the white man who was interested in Islam.

Bakayna Diakité (1920–1993), imam of Djenné from 1992 to 1993

Chapter 2

Two Kinds of Knowledge

"Welcome to Djenné. Did you have a good trip? How are my friends in Holland?" Boubakar shook my hand enthusiastically. The morning after my arrival in Djenné, I told the boys who always hang around the Hotel-Campement, hoping to snag a tourist in need of a guide, that I had a letter for Boubakar Kouroumansé. One of them dashed off to fetch him. In the Netherlands I had been told that Boubakar could help me find a house in Djenné and set up my research, since he had worked as an interpreter and assistant on an architectural project in Djenné carried out by students from the Eindhoven University of Technology.

Boubakar not only helped me find an apartment, fix it up, and furnish it—a task that occupied my daytime hours—but also took me to a number of evening gatherings where Qur'anic teachers and their students recited songs in praise of the Prophet.

A few days after my arrival, the city's peace and quiet was suddenly broken around 9:30 PM by the crackling of a public address system piping out distorted but melodious male voices. They seemed to be coming from the other side of the market square, and my first thought was that they were intoning the Qur'an. My inquiries revealed, however, that those snatches of sing-song blaring out into the city were not passages from the Qur'an but poems in praise of Muhammad. That evening marked the beginning of the third month of the Islamic year, the month in which the Prophet's birth and naming are commemorated. At two places in the city, marabouts were leading the first in a series of gatherings at which Arabic odes to the Prophet would be recited. Boubakar promised to take me to one of these gatherings, which would be held almost every evening up to the celebration of Muhammad's name day (*almudu*) on the eighteenth of the month.

21

I first attended a gathering of men singing the Prophet's praises a couple of days later. Lighting my path with a flashlight, I followed Boubakar through a maze of pitch-dark streets and alleyways as the drone of men's voices grew louder. We passed people sitting huddled up outside, their vague shapes dimly lit by the oil lamps in the doorways. Later I was told that they were women who had come outside to hear the recitations. At the end of the street I no longer needed my flashlight. Here the obscurity of the moonless evening was pierced by the glare of battery-powered fluorescent lights. We found ourselves standing at the edge of a small square in which a large group of men were seated.

Reed mats had been spread out to accommodate the listeners; we took a place among them at the back. I felt ill at ease, but apart from the boys sitting just behind us in the sand, who called to me softly in an attempt to get my attention, my presence did not cause much of a stir. Some of the men threw me furtive glances, and one or two asked Boubakar who his white companion was.

Facing one another in approximately the middle of the gathering were two groups, each consisting of about 20 "readers." The leader of each group had a microphone at his disposal; the groups took turns reciting several lines of text. Most of the readers were holding a book or manuscript, or had one lying before them on the ground. A loudspeaker mounted on a pole amplified the leaders' lilting tones. In a low voice, Boubakar pointed out the marabouts among the readers, and explained that the young men seated around them, joining in the recitation, were their advanced students. An old man holding a whip strolled among the boys in the outermost circle of listeners. When they got too rowdy, a threatening gesture was usually all that was needed to restore order.

Boubakar and I went to a number of these gatherings, including the closing almudu festival on Muhammad's name day, attended by hundreds of people who came to listen to the men reciting and to the marabouts telling of the Prophet's life.

*T*he apartment I rented consisted of two rooms opening onto a veranda. One was my bedroom and the other my study. Seated at the large table custom-made by a carpenter, Boubakar and I had long talks. At such times I often took notes, and one of the first things I wrote down was what he told me about himself and his family.

Boubakar, the son of Almamy Kouroumansé and Kadidya Tementao, was born in 1961 in the Yoboukayna quarter of Djenné. Almamy Kouroumansé—who, like his wife, belonged to the ethnic group of the Bozo—was a mason and fisherman, both traditional Bozo occupations.

Almamy taught these two trades to his sons (Boubakar was the younger of the two), so that later they would be able to earn a living. All the boys in Djenné are sent to a Qur'anic school at the age of seven or eight, and Boubakar was no exception. For seven years he was taught by a marabout to recite and write the verses of the Qur'an. In the mid-1970s he attended a madrasah in the city. At this small private school, which later became a state-financed *école franco-arabe*, he received instruction in reading, writing, and speaking the Arabic language, as well as lessons in arithmetic and the history of Islam. After three years at this school, he spent a year at a similar school in Mopti.

Having been born and raised in multiethnic Djenné, Boubakar had mastered—in addition to the rudiments of Arabic, which he had learned at the madrasah—a number of local languages. Besides Songhay, the *lingua franca* of Djenné, he spoke Bozo, the language of his ethnic group, Bamana, the *lingua franca* of Mali, and a bit of Fulfulde, the language of the Fulbe, who comprised some 20 percent of Djenné's population. Like most people his age, Boubakar had learned French from friends who attended the French *école fondamentale* in the city, and by listening to the radio.

When I was doing my fieldwork in the second half of the 1980s, Boubakar was still a bachelor. The youngest child in the family, he had lodgings of his own where he slept, but otherwise he was still a member of his parents' household. His two older sisters, Nakeydya and Fata, and his brother, Mahaman, were married and living elsewhere in the city. In the small, simple dwelling that housed his parents, his 80-year-old "grandmother" Ata (actually his paternal grandmother's sister), as well as two of Nakeydya's children, Boubakar took his meals and conducted his *tablier* trade. It was here that he had his "table" of wares—including cigarettes, candy, sugar, tea, dates, and kerosene—which he sold to local residents in an attempt to earn some money in the period of hardship following the drought of the early 1980s.

Another thing Boubakar and I talked about during those first few weeks were the religious festivities we attended together. I listed the marabouts' names, described the organization of the gatherings we attended, transcribed the titles of the Arabic books containing the odes that were recited, and recorded the customs surrounding the celebration of Muhammad's name day: Muhammad—whose name, Boubakar told me—should never be uttered without the accompanying blessing, "May God bless him and give him peace." My first notebook was rapidly filling up with information.

During one of these talks, I asked Boubakar if he would like to be my interpreter and research assistant. He agreed to this arrangement. After attending (and then discussing) the almudu gatherings, it had become clear to us both that Islam would be an important part of my research. Boubakar told me that if I wanted to study Islam, there were books I could consult: Arabic books in which scholars had recorded everything about the religion. Some people traveled to Egypt just to learn about Islam.

"Even about Islam as practiced in Djenné?" I asked.

"Yes, most certainly, Islam is the same everywhere," Boubakar replied, "but maraboutage," he went on to say, "is something else." And for that, it seemed, Djenné was the place to be.

Clearly, Boubakar made a distinction between "Islam" and "maraboutage," the latter term referring to the entire range of esoteric knowledge and practices in which marabouts specialize, including amulet-making and divination. And while Islam could be researched by reading books in Arabic—the language of the religion—maraboutage could be studied only "on location."

The dichotomy that emerged from Boubakar's description of the differences between doctrinal Islam and maraboutage parallels the distinctions often made by scholars among the range of religious ideas and practices found in various Islamic societies and communities. Obviously there is a difference between orthodox Islam and popular Islam, that is to say, between official Islamic doctrine as set down by scholars and local, popular Islam, which includes those conceptions and practices that differ from the formal rules but are adhered to by large segments of the population.

Such distinctions are questioned by anthropologists, in particular, since religious ideas and practices are never inherently orthodox or unorthodox, scriptural or popular. They can be labeled as such only from a certain perspective by those familiar with the official texts. Anthropologists, however, seek to describe Islam from the inside out and from the ground up. They focus their attention mainly on how certain groups of believers see Islam and the role their notions play in daily life. Moreover, deciding which standpoints are doctrinally sound is a task for theologians and not for researchers who view religion as a cultural system. In the anthropological approach to Islam, furthermore, merely identifying two disparate traditions is too simplistic, since the various layers of Islam are more strongly interwoven than such a model suggests. Anthropologists studying Islam in the Middle East have found it impossible—even there, in the Islamic heartlands—to observe Islamic practices that are "pure" and unaffected by local variants. Furthermore, a number of Islamic practices once seen as "atypical" and interpreted as local hybrids have often proved on closer inspection to be much more widely diffused. Anthropological studies of certain Islamic communities have made a point of analyzing the relationship between the one, universal Islam and the multiplicity of religious ideas and practices in the Islamic world as a whole. Such a study was carried out, for example, by the Dutch anthropologist Marjo Buitelaar (1993), whose description of the way Moroccan women celebrate Ramadan shows that local practices that differ from Islamic law are not necessarily at odds with it, and that a universal Islamic principle such as fasting still leaves room for local interpretation. Two other studies that illustrate the added value of the anthropological approach to Islam are those written by Robert Launay (1992) and Benjamin Soares (2005). Both evaluate Islam in local contexts—Launay in an urban neighborhood in northern Ivory Coast and Soares in the town of Nioro in Mali—and both contest the false dichotomy of orthodox and unorthodox Islam. Anthropological studies such as these elucidate the interaction between the universal Islamic tradition, historically anchored in the Arab Middle East, and local variations wrought by Islamic practice, thus illustrating the continual changes in the way Islam is lived, wherever it is professed.

How, then, does this great variety of religious ideas and practices fit into a single notion of "Islam"? It is sometimes suggested that Islam should be referred to in the plural, as "Islams," but most Muslims would contest this theological judgment, rightly pointing out that it is not up to anthropologists to make such assertions and emphasizing that Islam does in fact have a number of key tenets that are essential to the understanding of faith and practice within this religion.

Boubakar maintained that my study of Islam should begin by reading books in Arabic. Djenné, however, was the place to learn more about maraboutage. As an anthropologist unschooled in Arabic, I could only welcome his suggestion. Clearly, there was useful work to be done here. But I was not entirely happy with the role in which Boubakar had cast me. It was certainly not my intention to focus solely on maraboutage. To begin with, I wanted to know more about the organization of Qur'anic education, the celebration of religious holidays, the rituals surrounding birth, circumcision, marriage, death, and much, much more. Surely it would be unwise to betray at this early stage in my fieldwork too strong an interest in maraboutage, since people did not readily talk about the secrets of amulet-making or divination.

But whatever it was I hoped to discover about Islam in Djenné, it was vital to establish contact with the marabouts, since they would no doubt be my most important source of information. I therefore needed to gain admission to the world of the religious specialists. Together with Boubakar, I drew up a plan to visit every marabout with a Qur'anic school in the city, and to ask each one about his personal history and the history of his school.

"The marabout will be here in a minute," said Boubakar, after announcing our visit in the inner courtyard of Mamadou Waigalo's house. Together with one of the marabout's daughters, Boubakar had returned to the vestibule, where I was waiting. The girl unrolled the reed mat she had brought for us. It was Thursday, so there were no lessons. On every morning and afternoon of the week—except for all day Thursday, and Friday morning—there were dozens of young pupils in the vestibule, receiving instruction from Waigalo. Today their wooden writing boards were stacked up in the corner, bearing silent witness to their endeavors. A thick layer of sand on the floor of tamped-down earth and a copy of the Qur'an in a niche in the wall further testified to the educational function of this particular vestibule.

While waiting for the marabout I remained on my mat, gazing through the doorway to the world outside. A tourist with a camera was standing a short distance away. As he focused his telephoto lens on Waigalo's house, the neighborhood children crowded around him, as they always do in such situations. I wondered what he would think when he looked at his photograph and discovered a white man in the shadow of the vestibule.

Waigalo's house was often photographed. A picture of it can be found in numerous travel guides and books on adobe architecture. Situated at a fork in the road, the old house with its characteristic, tall façade formed the head of a small block of houses. The portico-like entrance, with two pilasters continuing upward as a feature of the façade, five crenellations on the edge of the roof, and little towers marking both corners of the façade—all elements characteristic of the architecture of Djenné—had been given beautiful, rounded shapes by the masons who applied a new layer of mud plaster every few years. It was a magnificent house, but in some places large chunks of plaster had fallen off the outside walls, exposing the old cylindrical mud bricks. Like many other houses in the city, Mamadou Waigalo's house was not in very good repair. Owing to the recent drought, many inhabitants had no money to maintain their houses, and the failed harvests had severely reduced the amount of chaff available to make sufficiently adhesive mud plaster. The crisis that had gripped the Sahel in the early 1980s had left its mark on Djenné's houses.

Mamadou Waigalo came into the vestibule and sat down, cross-legged, opposite us. Boubakar and I slid forward. With my head at a slight angle, and—as courtesy dictates—with my left hand holding my lower right arm, I shook Waigalo's hand. Boubakar did the same. We asked him how he was doing this morning. "I am peaceful. I praise

Two monumental houses. These houses represent the two most important types of façade in the city. (A) The house of the traditional chief of Djenné and example of a Tukulor façade. (B) Example of a Moroccan façade.

God," he answered. How had he slept? "Peacefully. May God be praised." How were the members of his family and the other people in his household? "There is nothing wrong with them. They are healthy. They praise God." Waigalo likewise asked after our welfare and that of our loved ones. In similar terms we told him there was nothing but peace in our immediate circle and that everyone praised God.

"Might we be allowed to ask several more questions?" we asked the marabout. "Certainly," he replied. I took up my notepad and pen, and—as Boubakar and I had agreed to do beforehand—we picked up the thread of our last conversation. While I was working up the notes of our previous visit to the marabout, new questions had arisen, as usually happened when Boubakar and I talked things over.

The words I addressed to the marabout were translated into Songhay by Boubakar, who then translated the marabout's answers into French. We returned to the history of Waigalo's family. Waigalo, who was in his mid-fifties, belonged to an old family of Qur'anic teachers. At least four generations had preceded him until he himself had begun to give instruction in the early 1970s. He claimed that around a hundred pupils attended his school, which was one of the largest in the city. Waigalo's adolescent son helped teach the youngest boys.

"Good morning," said an old woman who had appeared in the doorway. Keeping one foot on the mud threshold, she leaned forward and inclined her head in our direction. Obviously surprised to see us, she laughed and addressed the marabout. How was he this morning? Had he slept well? How was his wife? Was she in good health? And were his children all right? The question-and-answer routine of the salutation ritual was performed to rhythmic perfection. Both parties asked after the welfare of each other's families, neighbors, and acquaintances. Everyone, it seemed, was well. May God be praised.

The old woman asked who we were. Boubakar told her who his father was and which quarter he lived in. He went on to say that I was Dutch, that I had come to Djenné to learn about Islam and the history of the city, and that he and I had already visited a number of marabouts. The woman nodded and gave me a friendly smile. "May God grant you a good day," she said as she turned to go and greet other neighbors. Waigalo turned toward us, and we resumed our talk.

The marabout mentioned the names of several family members who had been Qur'anic teachers, and I duly made a note of them. After a short silence he suddenly asked me, rather cryptically, "If one divides all the knowledge that exists into two parts, what is one part of it?"

"I don't know," I answered, surprised by the question. I wondered what he was getting at.

"Correct," said Waigalo, " 'I don't know' is one part of all knowledge. 'I don't know' is the largest part of all the knowledge in the world. 'I don't know' can deepen knowledge. When one is ignorant of something, one asks others for help. Once upon a time, long ago, there lived in the land of the white people a man whose knowledge made him unique. Everyone was in agreement about this. When someone asked him which 'path' or branch of knowledge he knew best, the man replied, 'What I don't know is greater than what I do know.' "

Suddenly a shadow fell over the vestibule. A large sheep was standing in the doorway, blocking the light as it moved its impressive head this way and that. "Shoo, shoo!" the marabout called out, and gestured a couple of times toward the inner courtyard. The sheep jumped inside and then trotted on into the yard. Four more followed suit. They had finished their morning foraging in town.

Now that the subject of knowledge had been broached, Waigalo went on to tell us how it could be obtained: "To acquire knowledge, true knowledge, one needs six things." First of all, he explained, one had to be intelligent. Second, one had to thirst for knowledge, to crave it. "For example, if you did not have such a craving for knowledge," said the marabout as he looked me in the eye, "if you were not so eager to acquire it, you would not have found everything you have found thus far." Third, Waigalo went on to say, one needed perseverance. Fourth, one should, ideally, have the means to devote oneself to study, and not have to worry about earning a living. Fifth, one needed the personal consent or approval of a marabout. The teacher had to know that his pupil truly hungered after knowledge, and he had to want to teach that pupil. And sixth, one needed time, a great deal of time.

These six prerequisites to finding knowledge, Mamadou Waigalo explained, had been cited by Ali, the nephew and son-in-law of the Prophet Muhammad. All of this was clearly set forth in an Arabic book titled *Instruction to the Pupil.*

" *S*eek knowledge from the cradle to the grave" is one of the most frequently quoted utterances of Muhammad. According to the *hadîth*—the record of his words and deeds—the Prophet also said, "The ink of the scholar is worth more than the blood of the martyr" and "Seek knowledge even as far as China." The students at the advanced Qur'anic schools in Djenné who devote themselves to the study of traditional Islamic learning are called *talibé*—after the Arabic *talib*, which means "seeker of knowledge" or "student." Talibés come to the city from miles around in search of knowledge. When we asked marabouts about their achers, we often received the same reply. They told us who had taught them to read the Qur'an and with whom they had subsequently "read books," but the question as to where they *had* studied was not a valid one, they said, because they were *still* studying. Studying does not come to an end. The search for knowledge is a lifelong quest.

The French term *marabout* is derived from the Arabic *al-murabit*, the plural of which is *al-murabitun* ("Almoravids"), a reference to the soldier-monks who in the eleventh and twelfth centuries were responsible for the Islamization of the Berbers of the western Sahara. One meaning of murabit is a religious person. The local languages spoken in Djenné refer to marabouts in the following terms: *alfaa* in Songhay, *modibo* in Fulfulde, and *karamogo* or *mori* in both Bamana and Bozo. All these words have Arabic origins. Alfaa is derived from *al-faqih* (jurist). Modibo and mori are corruptions of the Arabic *mu'addib* (educator, teacher). Karamogo means "someone who can read," the prefix kara- coming from the Arabic *qara'a* (to read, recite). "Scholar," "teacher," "man of letters": each of these concepts presupposes the possession of knowledge. Marabouts thus have knowledge—two kinds of knowledge, to be precise.

"There are two kinds of marabouts," Boubakar explained as we made our rounds. "There are *sirri* marabouts and *bayaanu* marabouts. Sirri marabouts know the secrets of amulet-making and divination. They often work at night, because they don't give instruction like bayaanu marabouts. Bayaanu marabouts teach at Qur'anic schools during the day, so they have no time at night to practice sirri, though many of them have knowledge of it. They can't practice sirri every night, but they can make time for it on Wednesday and Thursday nights, since there is no school all day Thursday, or on Friday mornings. Moreover, bayaanu marabouts who have a teaching assistant—a younger brother, perhaps, or a son or an older pupil—are free to pursue sirri. They perform mara-boutage for others, and this enables them to earn more money than they can from teaching alone."

Boubakar translated bayaanu as "clear knowledge" and sirri as "secrets." Both are loan words from the Arabic. Bayaanu is the Songhay variant of *bayan* (clarity); sirri is the equivalent of *sirr* (secret). Bayaanu knowledge is obtained from the study of the Qur'an and religious doctrine, from the most elementary level to the most advanced. It is connected with education and belongs to the public domain. Bayan means "to bring something from the realm of vagueness to that of clarity," as written on the first page of an Arabic book read at the advanced Qur'anic schools in Djenné. Sirri is the esoteric knowledge of amulet-making and other occult techniques, such as divination. Knowledge of sirri can be used to pursue personal and worldly goals—such as the attainment of health, riches, and power—and can even be used with evil intent, whereas bayaanu knowledge aims to further the collective welfare, that is to say, the ultimate salvation of all believers.

In our talks about Islam, Boubakar sometimes used the terms *almis-limi* and *almumin*. These concepts, which were also borrowed from the Arabic, can be translated as "Muslim" and "believer." When I asked him the precise difference between the two, Boubakar suggested that I put this to a marabout. It was a good question to ask the next time we visited Alfa Baba Kampo, widely known for his bayaanu scholarship, who taught at the advanced level.

When we asked Kampo to explain the difference between a "Muslim" and a "believer," his answer was clear and concise. An almislimi, he explained, is someone who adheres to the five pillars of Islam: first, making the profession of faith that involves declaring that "there is no god but God and Muhammad is his Prophet"; second, performing the ritual prayers five times a day; third, paying the alms tax to benefit the poor and needy; fourth, fasting during the month of Ramadan; and fifth, undertaking a pilgrimage to Mecca, assuming one has the means to do so. In the case of almumin, Kampo explained, there are six articles of faith: a believer is a person who believes in the oneness of God, as stated in the profession of faith; who believes in all the prophets God has sent; who believes in all the books that God has revealed to the prophets; who believes that the angels, human beings, spirits, and demons were created by God; who believes that on the last day God will destroy the world, after which all people will be resurrected by Him; and who believes that everything that exists and everything that happens is the work and the will of God.

Thus the marabout described the foundation of Islam, for he had named the devotional precepts laid down by Islamic law and the religious doctrine derived from the Qur'an. The five pillars of Islam—*islam* means submission (to God)—constitute the five duties that every Muslim must fulfill. The six articles of faith (*iman*) comprise the core beliefs of Islam, and it is these that are at the very heart of bayaanu knowledge.

Sirri knowledge, on the other hand, is an entirely different matter. A young marabout once told us how difficult it was for him to support his wife and children, saying that sometimes they were barely able to make ends meet. The pupils at his Qur'anic school paid only a small tuition fee, and his plot of land—which he and his pupils cultivated, as did many marabouts in the city—had yielded little this year, even though the rainy season had been promising. All of a sudden, as though unexpectedly seeing a way out of his difficulties, he asked if the people in my country had any need of marabouts. And to recommend himself he began to list the things that marabouts could bring about with their knowledge of sirri: "They can help a man find a wife. Some men have no luck finding a wife, but marabouts can help them, just as they can help a woman find a husband. They can help people find jobs, people who have finished their studies but can't find employment. If there are 40 candidates for a single job, they can make sure that a particular person gets that job. And they can help people pass exams. They can also prevent factory workers from having accidents, and when there's a war they can protect people from bullets. And for those with money, marabouts can ensure that their wealth will increase." The marabout told me that if I knew people in Holland with such problems, I should simply send them to him, in Djenné.

*G*iven the differences between bayaanu and sirri, if we were to place the marabouts of Djenné at some point between the two—with the scholars and teachers of classical Islamic doctrine at one end of the spectrum and the specialists in the occult practices of maraboutage at the other end—most of them would be somewhere in the middle. If, as Boubakar said, bayaanu marabouts also have knowledge of sirri, then the two categories must overlap to some extent.

On the bayaanu side are the marabouts who teach their pupils at the Qur'anic schools "how to follow God." Here we find the scholars and teachers, generally esteemed for their religious knowledge, who are naturally recognized as marabouts by one and all. At the other end of the continuum, it is more difficult to say who is a marabout and who is not.

To be sure, there are marabouts in Djenné who are reputed to be highly knowledgeable about esoteric sciences, but there are also many who could best be described as "part-time marabouts": men, often elderly, who occasionally practice maraboutage—or, as it is known in Songhay, *alfaa terey* (literally, maraboutism)—sometimes for a small fee, and frequently for friends and relations. Boubakar was one of those who made use of their services now and then.

Once, when we were talking about the hard life of petty traders in Djenné, Boubakar said that a month or two earlier he'd gone a whole week without a single customer. When he told his mother that he didn't understand why business was so bad, she suggested consulting a marabout, saying, "When there is something you can't explain, you must ask the advice of a marabout." She had recommended Brahima Coulibaly, who could "read the *turaabu*." Until the end of the 1970s, Coulibaly had been both a farmer and a small-scale trader who sold kerosene from his home. When his business went bankrupt, he devoted himself to maraboutage, which he had occasionally practiced in the past. Boubakar took

25 francs and went to see Coulibaly.[1] Usually one gave more, but when Boubakar explained to the marabout that it was impossible for him to pay more just then, Coulibaly was very understanding. To find the answer to Boubakar's question, he set up the turaabu table. Boubakar was somewhat reassured by the outcome. The patterns discernible in the 16 "houses" of the turaabu had not pointed to a specific problem. Business was bad because a fair number of Djenné's residents were temporarily out of town. Many had left the city to help with the harvest; others were seeking work elsewhere. Trade had declined throughout the city.

On another occasion Boubakar told me that Seydou Tounkara, an old man who lived a couple of streets away, had once given him an amulet to help boost sales. "Tounkara has knowledge of maraboutage, but he is not actually known as a marabout," Boubakar explained. Whenever Tounkara passed Boubakar's little shop, he stopped to ask how things were going. One day he promised to make something for him, and returned a few days later with an amulet devised to stimulate business. Later on Boubakar gave the old man 250 francs.

Neither Brahima Coulibaly nor Seydou Tounkara would be generally recognized as marabouts, yet they have sirri knowledge that they occasionally put into practice. The existence in Djenné of many "part-time marabouts" like Coulibaly and Tounkara tends to blur the boundary. Whenever I asked how many marabouts were living in Djenné, I always received the same answer: not only did people claim not to know, but they said that no one could possibly know, because—they assured me—everyone in Djenné had some knowledge of maraboutage. Even if "everyone" is an exaggeration, it is clear that many possess a form of knowledge that belongs to the domain of the marabouts.

Note

[1] Amounts of money are given in CFA (Communauté financière d'Afrique) francs, the monetary unit used in former French West Africa. Its rate of exchange was coupled to the French franc; before devaluation in January 1994, 50 CFA francs = 1 French franc (worth 15 eurocents in today's currency). The following commodity prices give some indication of the value of the CFA franc in the mid-1980s: rice (1 kilo) = 250–300 francs; millet (1 kilo) = 150–175 francs; sugar (1 kilo) = 350–400 francs; kerosene (1 liter) = 275 francs. The daily wage of a mason was 1,500 francs, and the daily wage of a mason's helper was 500 francs.

Sarmoy Korobara (1913–1992), imam of Djenné from 1958 to 1992

Chapter 3

The Qur'an
and Other Books

"*Bâ, sî, mî, alîfu, lâmu, lâmu, ha.*" Little Salifou stared timidly at the ground as he recited his lesson: "*alîfu, lâmu, ra, hâye, mîmu, nûnu, alîfu, lâmu, ra, hâye, yâye, mîmu.*" Boubakar's young nephew, having reached the age of seven, had recently started going to the Qur'anic school. One afternoon, as we were drinking tea in the courtyard of Boubakar's parents' home, I asked Salifou what he had learned so far. Slightly embarrassed, he rattled off the very first letters taught at Qur'anic schools. Boubakar smiled encouragingly as he took the enamel teapot from the charcoal stove and poured a long, thin stream of cloyingly sweet tea into our small glasses. He prompted Salifou by whispering some of the letters, trying to discover what progress he had made. Salifou was unenthusiastic, however, and soon got up and disappeared through the gate to go in search of his friends.

A few days later, Boubakar and I visited the Qur'anic school run by Salifou's teacher. On the way there, we passed Bokary Tomou's school. Bokary's younger brother was sitting beside the entrance, embroidering. He seemed to be working on the front of a *grand boubou*, the flowing, wide-sleeved robe worn by both men and women. We greeted him from a distance. The drone of boys repeating their lessons wafted through the air. During our previous visit, 70-year-old Bokary Tomou had told us that his family's school was among the oldest in the city. Long ago, one of his ancestors, accompanied by a large number of pupils, had come from the "Arabian lands" to Djenné to settle down and establish a Qur'anic school. At this school, which had been passed down from father to son through many generations, Bokary Tomou taught about fifty pupils. Occasionally his younger brother or his cousin—a son of his father's brother—took over the lessons, but usually Bokary Tomou himself was present.

The school run by Salifou's marabout was around the corner from Tomou's. In the shadow at the foot of the wall across from the teacher's house—instruction was given in the vestibule only in the morning, when the sun was high in the sky—some thirty pupils were seated around the marabout. Salifou was in the inner circle, among the youngest, who sat closest to the teacher. They were reading aloud, each boy reciting his own text to himself. A few of them were using their index fingers to follow the Arabic letters on their writing boards.

Seated on a sheepskin and leaning against the wall, the teacher listened to the cacophony of children's voices. Whenever the sound died down, he urged them to read more diligently. Next to him lay a whip made of two pieces of nylon cord tied to a wooden handle. Seated further along the wall were several advanced pupils, reciting long passages from the Qur'an at a remarkable speed. From time to time they refreshed their memories by consulting their lesson boards, on which verses from the Holy Book were written in tiny letters.

Two pupils sat a short distance from the group. One of them was writing on a board, using a reed pen that he kept dipping into the inkpot beside him in the sand. A sheet from a loose-leaf Qur'an lay before him, protected by a piece of cardboard, for the Qur'an must never touch the ground. His eyes moved constantly between the Qur'anic text and his writing board. In a somewhat sloping hand, he slowly copied the verses onto the thin layer of clay he had smeared on his board earlier that day, which by now had dried into a hard, gray surface. The boy next to him, who had probably finished copying his lesson, sat there, watching.

As everywhere in Islamic West Africa, children in Djenné are entrusted at about the age of seven to marabouts who teach them to read God's words, or rather to recite them, because they do not learn the meaning of those words. Djenné has more than thirty-five schools offering elementary instruction in the Qur'an. Most of these schools are housed in the vestibule of the teacher's house. The number of pupils varies considerably from school to school. The teachers I asked quoted numbers ranging from a dozen to a hundred and more, but I usually saw no more than several dozen pupils in a school at any given time. The large majority of the pupils are boys, mostly between the ages of seven and twelve, though some are older. The girls who are sent to Qur'anic schools often stay just long enough to memorize the shorter *suras* (chapters) of the

Marabout Baba Toumagnon in the midst of the pupils at his Qur'anic school. (A) In the morning, lessons are given outdoors. (B) In the afternoon, lessons are given in the vestibule of the teacher's house.

Qur'an, after which they are expected to stay home and help their mothers with the household chores.

Qur'anic schools offer individual instruction; there are no classes. Pupils work their way through the Qur'an at their own speed. The teaching materials are simple. The older pupils, who are set to copying texts on boards, provide their own pens, which are made of reeds, and inkpots filled with ink made from a mixture of soot (scraped from cooking pots), gum arabic, and water. The younger pupils have only their wooden writing boards, on which the teacher or an advanced pupil writes passages from the Qur'an. Neither blackboards nor notebooks are used, and apart from the marabout's own Qur'an and one or two copies made available to the advanced pupils, there are no books. Each Wednesday the pupils bring their tuition fees in the form of one or more coins—depending on what their parents can afford—usually between 10 and 15 francs. On Islamic holidays the amount is raised slightly: at the beginning of a new year and on the Prophet's name day, to around 50 francs, and for the feast at the end of Ramadan and the Feast of Sacrifice, to as much as 200 francs.

Various stages mark the elementary Qur'anic instruction given in Djenné. The first three are *aliifu-aliifu* (*alif* is the first letter of the Arabic alphabet), *timiti-timiti* (derived from the Arabic word *matta*, meaning to

A pupil at a Qur'anic school places his writing board in the sun to dry after smearing a new layer of mud on it. When the boards are dry, new lessons can be written on them.

stretch), and *chow-koray* (literally, clean reading). In these stages the pupils learn the 28 letters of the Arabic alphabet, the way in which the different vowel signs and other orthographic marks determine pronunciation, and finally, how the letters are combined to produce words. The letters are learned in the order in which they occur in the Qur'an, beginning with the first sura—*al-Fatiha* (The Opening)—and continuing with the short suras at the end. By reducing the verses of the Qur'an to their smallest components—the letters—pupils learn to recognize and name all the letters of the Arabic alphabet. The letters that Salifou recited to me that afternoon form the words *Bismillah ar-rahman ar-rahim.* This line—"In the name of God, Merciful to all, Compassionate to each!"—opens the Qur'an and all but one of its suras.

The first letters of the Qur'an are not, however, the first letters written on the pupils' boards. When a new pupil is brought to school, a marabout begins by asking God to "open" that pupil's mind. To do this he makes use of the special powers attributed to the words of the Qur'an, which are said to contain *baraka,* God-given spiritual powers. It is these powers that are harnessed in the amulets made by marabouts. And just as words from the Qur'an are written in amulets made to serve a wide variety of purposes, a Qur'anic teacher writes a text, which is intended to "open the mind" of his new pupil.

This text, written once on the pupil's writing board and once on the palm of his hand, might consist of the standard formulas—"In the name of God, Merciful to all, Compassionate to each!" or "O God, bless our master Muhammad and the family of our master Muhammad and grant them peace," as well as such passages from the Qur'an as "My Lord, open my breast, make my mission easy for me, and untie the knot in my tongue, so that they may understand my speech" (20:25–28) or "We shall dictate it to you, and you shall not forget, save what God wishes" (87:6).[1]

The teacher writes the Qur'anic text on the palm of his pupil's right hand, and then orders him to lick it off. By licking off the ink, the boy absorbs the beneficent force contained in the words. The passages from the Qur'an that are used to "open the mind" of the beginning pupil—to make his mission easy, as one line says—explicitly refer to their purpose in this context. The skills needed by pupils to recite their lessons, such as memorizing what is dictated, are named in these passages.

The pupil not only assimilates the text by licking if off his palm, but also learns how to pronounce the words. The teacher declaims the text twice, and the pupil repeats it twice, pronouncing to the best of his ability words that are completely foreign to him.

For some pupils, the text meant to "open the mind" is not the first thing written on their boards. Sometimes a child of five or six is brought to school by an older sibling. A child considered too young for Qur'anic instruction is given a writing board on which the marabout has written Arabic texts such as "He likes chicken, he likes beef, he likes goat meat" or "He eats a meal and he drinks water and he sleeps a lot." Now and then the child is told how to pronounce the words written on his or her board. The youngest pupils are thus kept occupied with secular texts until they are old enough to come into contact with the words of the Holy Book.

*T*he Qur'anic lessons given to beginners use the shortest suras. Except for the first one, the 114 suras of the Qur'an are arranged according to length, the shortest ones appearing at the end of the book. Each of the first three stages of instruction begins with the first sura of the Qur'an, followed by the last ten suras, in reverse order. Pupils thus begin with the chapters that are the easiest to memorize, and continue to learn the Holy Book from back to front. The goal is to be able to recite the last verses of the second and longest sura, by which time the pupil will have "read" the entire Qur'an. Most pupils, however, leave Qur'anic school before getting this far.

The teaching method used in these first stages is as follows. The marabout writes a few letters, words, or verses on the pupil's board and

Baba Toumagnon listens to a pupil reciting his lesson.

reads them aloud in a way suitable to the child's level of learning. The pupil repeats the lesson, and continues to do so for as long as it takes to recite it perfectly. Every day the marabout listens to his pupils reciting their lessons individually. When he is convinced that a pupil can recite the text correctly, he gives that pupil permission to wash off the writing board. Advanced pupils must do this often. The youngest are given only a few letters at a time and therefore have to wash off their boards only once in a while.

For this purpose a special water jar is kept in the courtyard. Pupils balance their writing boards on the edge of the jar and wash off the side that was written on first, the one with the penultimate lesson. The water used to do this is carefully caught in the jar and saved. Once or twice a year the jar is taken outside the city to be cleaned. The water it contains—by now black and muddy from all the ink and clay—is emptied into an open body of water and the jar is then rinsed out. Its contents must not be emptied in an unclean place, for the water contains the words of God and must therefore be handled with care. The jar used to wash off the writing boards is called *nesi-kusu*: *kusu* means "jar" and *nesi* can be translated as "amulet-water." Sometimes, Boubakar said, people

Three pupils at a Qur'anic school washing their writing boards. The jar (nesi-kusu) holds the water that contains the power of the Qur'anic texts dissolved in it. On the left, a pupil scatters mud granules on his writing board. The boy on the right rubs the mud over his board.

come to fetch water from a Qur'anic school's nesi-kusu to use at home for medicinal purposes, since water containing God's Word is thought to have therapeutic properties.

The chow-koray stage of "clean reading" lasts until the sixty-eighth chapter of the Qur'an. The sura *al-Qalam* (The Reed Pen) marks the end of the first half of elementary instruction in the Qur'an. After this, the pupil is taught not only to read the words of the Qur'an, but also to write them. Using a sharpened piece of wood, the marabout scratches the verses into the thin layer of clay smeared on the board, after which the pupil carefully fills in the scratched lines with ink. This stage is called *khairun* (from the Arabic *khair*, meaning good or blessing). At some schools this is followed by another stage, called *khairun qasida* (from the Arabic *qasida*, meaning correct or without mistakes), during which the marabout leaves bigger spaces between the lines, and pupils no longer fill in the writing, but copy it themselves below the teacher's example.

By the end of the khairun stage, the pupils have "read" one-fourth of the Qur'an. They are then required to copy the remaining chapters on their own, without having the teacher's example to follow. Qur'anic

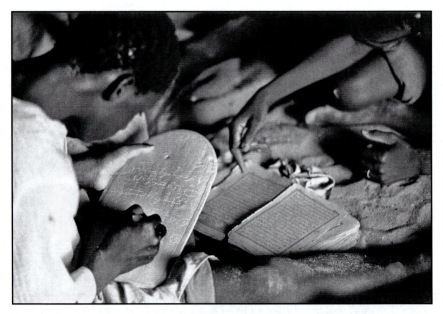

Lessons in writing begin during the khairun stage of education at a Qur'anic school. Using a sharpened piece of wood, the teacher—or in this case an older, more advanced pupil—scratches the Qur'anic text into the layer of mud covering the writing board. Pupils learning to write the Arabic script then use pen and ink to fill in the lines written by the teacher.

schools thus have several loose-leaf copies of the Qur'an, from which pupils in the *fita* stage (fita means sheet or page) borrow pages to copy. When the fita pupil has finished transcribing his lesson, he gives his writing board to the marabout, who corrects his mistakes and teaches him how to pronounce the words. This stage, which comprises the largest part of the Qur'an, ends with the last verses of the second sura, *al-Baqara* (The Cow).

A special ceremony is held for a pupil who has worked his way through the entire Qur'an. The father of the boy gives the teacher a sum of money, and other Qur'anic teachers are invited to the school to witness the pupil reciting twice over, as he repeats his teacher's words, the last part of the second sura. After this, one or two of the visiting marabouts pronounce blessings, and all those present partake of a meal offered by the pupil's parents. Then the boy and some of his schoolmates walk around town, collecting small gifts. Going from door to door, he cries out "*Alkorana albarka!*" ("The beneficent force of the Qur'an!") and proudly displays his writing board.

Most of the marabouts I asked said that it takes at least four years to "read" the entire Qur'an by completing the various stages of instruction at a Qur'anic school. But, they hastened to point out, many pupils take longer and most never get this far.

*T*he Qur'an is first and foremost a book intended for recitation. Qur'an means, in fact, "recitation." The opening of the ninety-sixth chapter—the sura with which, according to some traditions, the revelation of God's Word to Muhammad began—reads as follows: "Recite, in the name of your Lord! He Who created!" It is mainly as a recited text that the Qur'an looms large in the daily life of Muslims. The Holy Book is the common property of all believers. Regardless of one's social standing, level of education, or ability to understand Arabic, no Muslim can function—either in the ritual prayer of the *salât* or in personal devotion—without being able to recite a minimum of the Arabic text of the Qur'an. The recitation of the Holy Book, in which a deep respect for the Word of God is expressed, is at the very core of the Islamic faith.

In Djenné, too, the Qur'an is recited and listened to. At funerals, the male mourners recite large parts of the Holy Book. During the night in which God's revelation to Muhammad is commemorated—the Laylat al-Qadr in the month of Ramadan—readers at a dozen Qur'anic schools recite the entire Qur'an in one long session. And every morning and afternoon during Ramadan, a large audience listens to the tafsîr readings at a number of places in the city.

Reciting the words of the Holy Book is a religious and devotional exercise in itself; understanding their meaning is far less important. The language of the recitations—classical Arabic—is the language of divine revelation. By reciting the words of the Qur'an, a meaning is conveyed that transcends their literal significance. As at all Qur'anic schools in the Islamic world, pupils in Djenné are instructed in the ritual recitation of the Qur'an. Learning to read the Qur'an, even without understanding a single word of it, is in itself an indispensable religious exercise.

At the elementary Qur'anic schools in Djenné, pupils do not learn to read or write in the usual sense. Instruction does not lead to literacy. A pupil does not learn how to read a text; he learns how to read The Text. Only after becoming acquainted with the language of God's Word—by reciting first letters, then words, and finally sentences—does he learn how to write that language. During their entire time at a Qur'anic school, pupils are never told the meaning of the words they are taught. Given neither translations nor explications, they are expected only to recite those words correctly and to write them without error.

*T*he experiences of Boubakar's young nephew Salifou and his fellow pupils—who attend Qur'anic school twice a day, but eat and sleep at home—are a far cry from the deprivations suffered by the many garibus who come to stay in Djenné at certain times of the year.

Daouda Gindo and his pupils, for example, were away from home for two to three months a year. They used to go to Burkina Faso, but when a border conflict with Mali in early 1986 made this impossible, they started coming to Djenné instead. Daouda Gindo was a Dogon from a village about one hundred kilometers east of Djenné. He was a marabout, and along with ten of his young Qur'anic pupils, including his own son, he had come to the city to devote himself to his studies. Together with an acquaintance—another Dogon marabout who had been living for years in Djenné—he was studying the secrets of maraboutage, but he also had pupils whom he instructed in the reading of the Qur'an. More than twenty-five years earlier, Gindo—then 20 years old—had spent some time in Djenné with his marabout. The same landlord who at that time had provided accommodation to Gindo's marabout now provided Gindo and his pupils with simple lodgings, asking no money for two small rooms in an unoccupied, dilapidated house. The man was doing it "for God." Otherwise the pupils saw to their own upkeep as well as that of their teacher.

Gindo's pupils were garibus. Three times a day, at mealtimes, they made the rounds with their begging bowls. Some of them had a gourd in

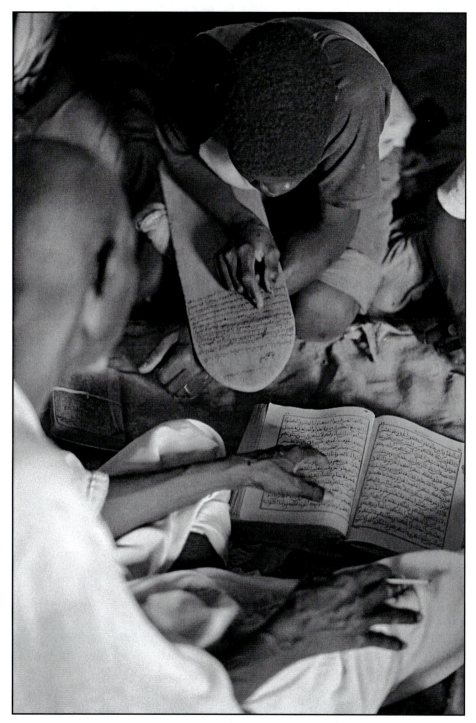

Baba Toumagnon and a pupil read a text aloud together, to check what the pupil has just written; the pupil reads from his writing board, the teacher from the Qur'an.

which to collect food, others an old tin can or a small plastic pail. Each boy had his own route. They stopped at every door, calling out "Friend of God, here is a stranger!" and waiting for a reply. If they heard, "May God grant you good fortune, stranger," they knew there was nothing to be had, and simply continued on their way. But if they were called into the inner courtyard, they would be given a handful of millet, rice with a bit of sauce, or whatever was being served that day. "May God accept it," they wished their benefactors.

As the donations mounted and their meal became more and more of a hodgepodge, Daouda Gindo's pupils continued to go from door to door. "Friend of God, here is a stranger" regularly resounded in the streets. When a pupil had collected enough to eat, he returned to his teacher, put down his begging bowl, and waited until his fellow pupils had returned. When they were all present, and Gindo had served himself from the bowls, the pupils finally began to eat.

Except for all day Thursday and Friday morning, a typical day in the life of Daouda Gindo's pupils went something like this: their first waking hour, just after sunrise, was devoted to learning the passages from the Qur'an written on their boards. After this, between 7:00 and 8:00 AM, they left to go begging, and around 8:30, when they had all returned to their humble lodgings, they had breakfast. For the rest of the morning, Gindo concentrated on his own studies, and his pupils wandered about the city. If possible, they earned a bit of money doing odd jobs. At noon they went begging for their midday meal, and after the 2:00 PM prayer, they resumed their lessons. Around mid-afternoon Gindo listened to each pupil reciting his assigned passage. Those who had learned their lessons well were allowed to wash off their writing boards, after which they were given new passages and told how to read them. Then they went on studying until about 4:30 PM. In the evening, after begging from door to door and eating their evening meal, they resumed their lessons. Sitting by a kerosene lamp or studying by the light of the moon, they continued to drone passages from the Qur'an until around 10:00 PM.

After two months in Djenné, Daouda Gindo and his pupils returned to their native village in early June to help with the crops. There were fields to be plowed and seeds to be sown before the rains came. A small procession left the city, the teacher riding on a donkey cart along with the baggage—each pupil had a small bundle of clothing and a writing board—and the pupils following on foot behind. Gindo told Boubakar that their journey would take five days.

"The Qur'anic school is the place where children learn obedience, where they get a good education," Boubakar once said to me. Not long before this, we had happened to pass a school where a pupil was being punished for truancy. As he lay face down, four of his schoolmates picked him up by his arms and legs and held him up off the ground while the marabout cracked the whip, hard, on his back and upper legs. We heard the boy's screams, and as we continued on our way, Boubakar told me that the truant's father or another relative might well have brought him to the marabout to be punished in this way.

This was the severest punishment I witnessed at a Qur'anic school, but the whip is not reserved for truants: pupils who fail to learn their lessons are also threatened with it. Indeed, a whip made of rope, nylon, or leather is part of the Qur'anic teacher's standard equipment. A pupil who is not diligent or repeatedly makes mistakes can count on a few well-aimed blows, or at least the threat of them, which is often enough to make him work harder. Boubakar told me he had once heard a marabout say that any body part that is struck at a Qur'anic school will not end up in hell, while in paradise the places touched by the whip will be "like jewels on the body."

When a pupil is first brought to a Qur'anic school, he is "given" or "handed over" to his teacher. Parents who entrust their child to a marabout therefore allow that marabout to assume responsibility for the child's education. They would never try to interfere with the marabout's methods, not even to temper the severity of a punishment. Nor are severe punishments meted out only at Qur'anic schools: in daily domestic life corporal punishment is also a generally accepted practice. A stick or a rope is considered a suitable means of correcting a disobedient child.

The instruction given at elementary Qur'anic schools does not confine itself to reciting God's Word and acquiring the rudiments of reading and writing. The Qur'anic school is considered an important formative experience, for it trains pupils to be obedient, respectful, and humble, thus acquainting them with important aspects of Islamic social life.

When I returned to Djenné in June 1987 after spending several months at home in the Netherlands, I discovered that I had new neighbors. The woman who had been living with her two small daughters in the rooms downstairs had found other lodgings nearby, and three advanced Qur'anic students had taken their place. The sounds coming from downstairs had changed: instead of infants crying, there were now male voices droning Arabic texts.

The three students, the oldest of whom was around thirty and the other two perhaps seventeen, came from a village around two hundred kilometers north of Djenné. Yousouf Traoré, the oldest of the three, was studying Arabic grammar at a Qur'anic school for advanced instruction. On two previous occasions he had come to the city as a talibé, the first time for a year, the second time for six months. The two younger pupils were in Djenné for the first time. Yousouf was instructing them in the first subjects studied at the advanced level. In their native village they had read the Qur'an, but now they wished to continue their studies, and had begun to read books on Islamic jurisprudence.

There were many talibés like Yousouf Traoré in the city. Even though Djenné's glorious days as a hub of Islamic scholarship belong to the past, the city is still of regional importance as a center of Islamic learning. In addition to the many elementary Qur'anic schools (*tirahuu*), Djenné has about ten schools for advanced Islamic education. At these "book schools" (a literal translation of the Songhay term *kitaabu-tirahuu*) or *majlisus* (from the Arabic *majlis*, meaning gathering), advanced students receive instruction in traditional branches of Islamic studies (after learning how to "read" the Qur'an at the elementary level). Under the supervision of a marabout, they read the works of classical Muslim authors in such fields as jurisprudence (*fiqh*), Arabic—including grammar (*nahw*), orthography (*rasm*), conjugations (*tasrîf*), prosody (*ʿarûd*), style and rhetoric (*balâgha*), and literature (*lugha*)—theology (*tawhîd*), the traditions of the Prophet (hadîth), panegyrics to the Prophet (*madîh*), mysticism (*tasawwuf*), the art of recitation (*tajwîd*), and Qur'anic exegesis (tafsîr). In most cases a majlisu is part of a larger Qur'anic school, where elementary instruction is also given. While the father instructs pupils in "books," his son gives lessons in reading the Qur'an.

The great majority of Djenné's advanced students come from outside the city, mostly from villages in the region of the Niger's Inland Delta. Some of them remain in the city for years; others return to it periodically. During the agricultural season, especially at harvest time, many students must return to their native villages to work in the fields. Depending on the time of year, between 200 and 250 talibés were staying in Djenné in the second half of the 1980s. Several dozen of them had young pupils of their own, also from other places, to whom they gave lessons in reading the Qur'an or, as Yousouf Traoré did, in the first subjects taught at the advanced level.

One marabout summed up the course of traditional Islamic education in Djenné as follows: "As children we read the Qur'an, without concerning ourselves with its meaning. Children aren't yet able to distinguish between good and bad. They're too playful for that. We read the Qur'an all the way through—once, twice, or three times—after which we can begin to study books. We read books until we understand them. Finally, after reading a great many books, we return to the Qur'an and read exegetical commentaries. The words of God are 'heavy.' It is essential first of all to understand what the religion signifies, to know how to follow God, before concerning ourselves with the meaning of the words in the Qur'an."

While the study of Qur'anic exegesis (tafsîr) is undertaken at the end of a course of advanced education, jurisprudence comes at the very beginning. The first books that a pupil learns to read almost always deal with fiqh (Islamic jurisprudence), or the science of law. It is often said that Islamic Law (*Sharia*)—which is founded on the divine principles revealed in the Qur'an and the sayings and deeds of the Prophet Muhammad (*Sunnah*)—is a "doctrine of duties," that is to say, a collection of precepts, a code of conduct for the individual Muslim. It sets forth the status of individuals in society, their rights and duties, as well as their prospects of heavenly reward or eternal damnation. Fiqh books thus deal not only with such subjects as marriage, divorce, inheritance, trade, wrongful acts, and theft, but also with prayer, ritual cleanliness, uncleanness, fasting, and dietary laws. Both social and devotional precepts have a place in Islamic law, and both are treated in the same way. Fiqh books examine the conditions that prayer must fulfill to be valid, the rules regarding fasting, and the procedure for paying the alms tax. By reading these books, students at the majlisus in Djenné learn the religious rules that dictate "how one must follow God."

Still, students embarking on advanced studies are not primarily concerned with the contents of the books they read. Acquiring knowledge of the Arabic language is more important. By reading books under the supervision of a teacher who translates them word for word, students gradually gain a deeper understanding of Arabic. Only at a later stage do they begin to study the language systematically by concentrating on Arabic grammar and linguistics. After that, when they have a reasonable command of Arabic, advanced students will often reread the fiqh books they read at the beginning of their studies.

*O*ne morning we visited the school where Yousouf Traoré received instruction from his marabout, Allaye Diallo. That morning Boubakar came to fetch me early, since the lessons began before 6:30 AM. We walked through the town, which was slowly waking up, to the quarter in which Diallo lived. The sun had just risen above the houses on the east side of the city, bathing everything in a soft light. We passed the first pupils carrying writing boards, trudging sleepily to their Qur'anic schools. From inner courtyards came the sound of mortar and pestle. Boubakar stopped a couple of times in an open doorway to shout good morning, and received greetings in return. At the edge of the market square, vendors were unbolting the heavy iron doors of their shops and warehouses. Several garibus, clutching their begging bowls, stood on a corner, undecided as to which route to take. A girl who had gone to fetch fire from her neighbors stepped cautiously over a high threshold, taking care not to let the glowing coals fall off her slotted spoon. A bit further on, a door flew open and hisses were heard as sheep were chased out of a house and into the street.

We arrived at Diallo's to find him with seven pupils. The reed mats had already been placed in the vestibule. Diallo sat in his usual place with his back against the wall. One pupil sat across from him, the others a short distance away. A book on Arabic grammar lay open on the mat between teacher and pupil. Bending over, with his legs folded beneath him and his head resting on his left arm, the young man ran his right index finger over the lines Diallo was reading aloud. The marabout paused every few words to translate the Arabic into Fulfulde, speaking both languages in the same monotone, so that it was difficult for the unpracticed ear to hear where the text left off and the translation began.

The other pupils waited until it was their turn to take their book and sit opposite the teacher. Some were reading, others listening to Diallo's reading and translation. Between 6:30 and 9:00 that morning, 16 pupils ranging in age from 14 to 40 received instruction from Diallo. Most of these lessons lasted just under ten minutes.

The pupil seated across from Diallo closed his book and got up. He found a place among the others and began silently rereading the passage Diallo had just translated for him. A boy of about fifteen slid forward and took his place opposite the teacher. Before opening his book, he placed a 100-franc coin next to the other coins on Diallo's mat. It was Wednesday, and these advanced students—like the pupils at elementary Qur'anic schools—had brought their voluntary donation for the teacher. Meanwhile, Yousouf had walked into the vestibule, accompanied by a friend with whom he often studied. Another student, whose lesson had taken place earlier, left the school and began to look for his shoes among those standing next to the door.

The young student was seated across from Diallo for less than three minutes. He was one of the youngest in the school, and had only recently begun his studies at the advanced level. Every day Diallo took two or three lines of the boy's book on fiqh and translated them into Songhay, the language of Djenné, for unlike most of his fellow pupils, the boy was actually a native of Djenné. In contrast to the method Diallo employed with his advanced students, to whom he read and translated the texts without a break, when teaching this boy he paused every couple of words to give him a chance to repeat both the Arabic text and its translation. Reading Arabic was no problem for the boy, since he had studied for years at the Qur'anic school. But no one had ever told him the meaning of those Arabic words. Now, for the first time, he was discovering what they meant.

When it was Yousouf's turn, he showed the teacher where they had stopped the previous day. Diallo glanced at the book, which lay upside down in front of him, and began almost immediately to read and translate. It was a fiqh book. Years before, Yousouf had read most of it without really understanding it. But now that he had studied a number of books on Arabic grammar, he had decided to reread it.

Yousouf paid close attention as Diallo translated the sentences for him. A couple of hours later, he would recite them again at home. As they did almost every day, two of his fellow pupils, who were reading the same book, would drop in, and while I worked on my notes with the help of Boubakar, I could hear the talibés downstairs, reciting their lessons.

*O*ver the years Yousouf himself took on various pupils, all of whom came from his native village or its immediate vicinity. One exception was Mamadou, a young Dogon, six or seven years old at the most, whose marabout had left him with Yousouf. Mamadou's marabout, also a Dogon, had studied for a time with Yousouf, but when he had to return to his family to help with the harvest, he asked Yousouf to take Mamadou under his wing. Two of Yousouf's advanced pupils, both about twenty, had taken charge of Mamadou. They devoted themselves to teaching him the rudiments of Qur'an-reading by acquainting him with Arabic letters. When passing through the vestibule downstairs, I repeatedly saw little Mamadou in a corner, holding his writing board on his lap and reciting his lessons. An older pupil, who was poring over a book in Arabic, corrected Mamadou whenever he heard him make a mistake.

Both Yousouf and his other pupils were Bamana, and because many Fulbe lived in their native region, they all spoke Fulfulde as a second language. Mamadou spoke only Dogon and a smattering of Fulfulde. Neither Yousouf nor his other pupils had any knowledge of Dogon. I tried not to think about how difficult it must have been for little Mamadou to be surrounded, day in and day out, by people unfamiliar with his language. But I couldn't help wondering how his lessons were going, considering the scant communication between teacher and pupil. Boubakar, however, thought nothing of it. All Mamadou had to do, after all, was repeat *bâ*, *sî*, *mî*, and so on, and by way of illustration, Boubakar picked up the can of Lipton Tea from the table on the veranda and ran his finger across the label, pronouncing each letter in turn: "L-i-p-t-o-n." Surely that was clear. A Qur'anic pupil was expected to repeat the letters he was prompted to say, and that was all. Only at the advanced level was it necessary for teacher and pupil to understand each other. That's when explanations were given, not at the elementary level.

Another young pupil who lived downstairs was Saadou, a boy of seven or eight whose father had entrusted him to Yousouf, a distant relative, to teach him to read the Qur'an. Together with two boys of about nineteen, Saadou had traveled to Djenné from his native village. He received some of his lessons from Yousouf's older pupils, who wrote the Qur'anic verses on his board and told him how to pronounce them. A couple of evenings a week, Yousouf listened to him reciting his lessons. Saadou was trying to memorize large parts of the Qur'an, so everything he learned to read, he learned by heart at the same time.

One evening toward the end of 1990, my girlfriend Nan and I were lying on the bed, reading. It was the first time she had come to Djenné, where I had lived for more than a year and a half in the days before we'd met. A dim circle of light hovered around the flame of the kerosene lamp hanging on the wall at the head of the bed. The rest of the room lay in darkness. The door to the veranda was open, as always, to let in the cool night air. From downstairs came the sound of Saadou's voice, rattling off Qur'anic verses.

Now and then Saadou's droning was interrupted by the voice of Yousouf, correcting him in harsh tones. From time to time Yousouf's admonitions were followed by the sound of a whip cracking and Saadou's suppressed cries. Sobbing, he resumed his recitation. I could tell that Nan was getting more and more upset. With a sigh of exasperation, she turned around on the uncomfortable straw mattress and tried, unsuccessfully, to concentrate on her book. I knew that she would have liked nothing better than to go downstairs and tell Yousouf exactly what she thought of his teaching methods. I wanted to tell her that Saadou was now assured of wearing "jewels" on his body when he entered paradise, but all I could manage was a clumsy apology: "That's just the way they do things here."

Still, was I any better at ignoring the situation? The question kept bothering me. Each of Saadou's sobs left a chip in my cultural-relativist veneer. At college it had all looked so good: anthropologists embrace the riches of other cultures, and accept them as they are. Ethnocentric judgments are totally unacceptable. I had no choice but to lie there, listening, as the Holy Word floated in tearful tones into the silence of the night.

Note

[1] The passages from the Qur'an are quoted from the English translation by Tarif Khalidi (Penguin Books, 2008).

Allaye Abaré Landouré (ca. 1913–1998)

Chapter 4

Invoking God

*O*nce, on our way to see the marabout Abdoulaye Touré, Boubakar suddenly asked if I wanted to meet "the female marabout." Long before this he had told me about Maimouna Niafo, who gave lessons to Djenné women who wished to study the Qur'an and books on Islam. Her name had come up when Boubakar was telling me about a certain woman his oldest sister and grandmother consulted whenever they had a question about prayer, particularly the correct way to perform the prayers said in addition to the ritual prayers performed five times daily by all observant Muslims. Their advisor was a pupil of "the female marabout."

It is well known that the researcher's gender is an important variable in many contexts in anthropological fieldwork. Although gender is only one of several personal characteristics that shape the dynamics of participant-observation and fieldwork relations, male ethnographers sometimes have difficulty crossing gender barriers and often face restrictions in interviewing women or observing female activities. In particular, when their research involves a society with strong gender-segregation traditions, the male anthropologist's position in the field can certainly distort his findings.

Just after replying that yes, I would very much like to meet "the female marabout," we stopped in front of the entrance to a house. Boubakar took off his slippers, as is customary before entering a Qur'anic school, and I followed his example. We went into the vestibule, where a small group of women were sitting on mats. Another woman, seated slightly further away, had several books at her side. The scene was similar to those I had observed in the schools for advanced Qur'anic instruction. Boubakar addressed the woman sitting apart from the others, telling her that we had come to pay our respects and introducing me by sketching my reasons for being in Djenné. Then he turned to me and said that this was Maimouna Niafo, the woman whose name had cropped up in our conversations. We over to her, squatted down, shook her hand, and seated ourselves beside her on the mat. Having arrived so unexpectedly, I wasn't sure what to do. Boubakar, too, was obviously ill at ease, and didn't really know how to handle the situation. Just when it occurred to me that we ought to ask her the same questions we usually asked the male marabouts we visited, Boubakar announced that it was time for us to go. We said our good-byes and, having stayed only a few minutes, left the vestibule where Maimouna Niafo continued to teach her pupils.

Outside, neither of us said a word about the visit. As we walked in the direction of Abdoulaye Touré's neighborhood, I remembered how Maimouna Niafo had been briefly mentioned, though not by name, during a visit to Alfa Baba Kampo. I had asked Boubakar to ask Kampo if there were any female marabouts in Djenné. A smile had appeared on Kampo's face, and he had quickly asked a question in return: What had made me think that? It was just as well that he gave me no time to answer, since it might have taken me a while to come up with a reply that met with Boubakar's approval. After all, it would not be proper to let the marabout know that Boubakar and I had already discussed the subject. Kampo's reply was curt and categorical—"Female marabouts don't exist. Only men can be marabouts"—as though that settled the matter and we could now move on to another topic.

Kampo's answer left us in no doubt: a "female marabout" was a contradiction in terms, at least according to the prevailing male discourse. And it was this discourse in which Boubakar and I found ourselves, and to which we were bound: otherwise relations with our interlocutors and our own collaboration would be jeopardized.

*H*aving arrived at the square on which Abdoulaye Touré lived in three different houses—one for each of his wives—we met one of his young daughters at the water tap. When we asked her if she knew where her father was that day, she disappeared into the nearest vestibule and quickly returned, pointing at the house where the marabout could be found.

"The marabout is upstairs," said Touré's first wife, who was in the courtyard, preparing the midday meal with the help of a servant and one of her daughters. Millet was being crushed in a mortar and the flour sieved above a large calabash. Halfway up the stairs we announced our arrival and heard someone call, "Welcome, do come in."

In the room on the other side of the landing at the top of the stairs, Touré sat on a thin mattress, reading a book in Arabic. Beside him was the large briefcase he always had with him; it was bulging with books, notebooks, papers, and—I couldn't help noticing—a flashlight. We sat down opposite the marabout on a mat woven with colorful strips of plastic. The cement floor felt cool. A large part of the room, whose walls were painted a pale blue, was taken up by a double bed. Stacks of books lay behind the sliding glass doors of the cupboard at the foot of the bed. Against the wall was a low cabinet also piled high with books. Several framed photographs were hanging above the bed: two color reproductions of the holy places in Mecca—souvenirs of the pilgrimages Touré had made in the early 1970s—and a black-and-white photograph of him as a young man, together with two of his brothers.

We exchanged greetings, asking the marabout if he and his loved ones were in good health, after which it was his turn to inquire after our welfare and that of our families. I was just about to request, as usual, permission to ask him some questions, and was expecting his customary reply— that he would tell us what he knew but not what he didn't know—when he reached into his briefcase and took out an envelope. This letter had just arrived, he said. Would I be so kind as to read it aloud?

I began to read the short letter, which was written in French, pausing after every few words to give Boubakar time to translate the French into Songhay. The marabout listened to Boubakar's translation while fanning himself with a fold of the tunic that enveloped his bulky shape. The letter, which had come from Bamako, contained a request to help a man get a job with a company in Ouagadougou, the capital of the neighboring country of Burkina Faso. The letter-writer mentioned the name of the company and its director, as well as the dates of the two selection rounds.

Suddenly a little boy appeared in the doorway, having climbed the stairs soundlessly. I stopped reading. Judging by his features, he was one of the marabout's many children. Not so long ago, Boubakar and I had visited one of Touré's wives to admire his youngest offspring. At the age of 64, he had become a father yet again.

Touré looked up, annoyed, and asked the child what he wanted. The boy was embarrassed, but approached his elderly father and told him shyly that his mother needed some money.

"What for?" the marabout asked.

'To buy some meat at the market," the boy said softly.

Touré felt around in the inside pocket of his robe, handed the boy a few coins and, gesturing with the same insouciance, sent him on his way.

I read the last lines of the letter. Touré took a ballpoint pen out of his bag, picked up the empty envelope, and asked me to repeat the names and dates. As I did so, he wrote down the information in Arabic and told us that the man who had sent the letter was no stranger to him. In fact, he already had his dossier—Touré used the French term—having previously received the necessary details from him.

In the letter I was reading aloud, the man from Bamako asked the marabout to "pray" for him, using the word *prier*. Boubakar translated *prier*, hesitantly but correctly, as *jingar*—which in Songhay means "to pray" in the sense of performing Islamic ritual prayer—but Touré found this amusing. "Jingar?" he laughed. "You mean *gaara!*"

Later that day I asked Boubakar to explain the difference between jingar and gaara. We had sometimes discussed these concepts, but they had been so emphatically contrasted during our visit to Abdoulaye Touré that I felt the need to bring the subject up again. "Jingar is obligatory, gaara is not," Boubakar said tersely, and added that jingar was subject to strict rules, but there were no rules governing gaara. In Arabic, jingar was *salât*, whereas gaara was *du͎â'*.

$\mathcal{T}$he language situation in which Boubakar and I worked was complex. Apart from the few cases in which Bamana was spoken, our talks with the marabouts took place in Songhay. As my fieldwork advanced, I was increasingly able to understand the gist of a conversation in Songhay, but Boubakar's services as an interpreter remained indispensable. In my notebook I recorded key words and short sentences in both French and Dutch. Later I worked up my notes, writing in detail in Dutch. Often I did this together with Boubakar. Discussing these matters in French, we were frequently confronted with the fact that French was neither his nor my mother tongue. I asked Boubakar to repeat characteristic phrases in Songhay, so that I could record them in that language too, along with the French translation. I looked up some of the words in a 1917 Songhay–French glossary, which I had once photocopied at the Utrecht University Library. Moreover, I made a habit of asking Boubakar the Arabic equivalent of certain Songhay words, certainly those expressing key religious concepts. We then looked up these terms in an Arabic–English dictionary. Knowing the Arabic terminology made it possible for me to search for more detailed definitions in standard reference works such as *The Encyclopaedia of Islam*, once I was back in the Netherlands.

Gaara was one of the concepts that occurred in my notes in a variety of languages. Gaara, which Boubakar always translated as *bénédiction* (or *bénir*, when used as a verb), is the Songhay term for the Arabic word du͎â'. This is illustrated by the Bamana and Fulfulde terms, which I also recorded in this context. Gaara in Songhay is the equivalent of *duwawu* in Bamana and *duao* in Fulfulde, both of which are clearly Arabic loan words.

According to the dictionary, du͎â' means "call, invocation of God, supplication, prayer, request, plea." The term "petitionary prayer" is also used in publications on this subject. Dictionary translations, however, are not the first translations sought by anthropologists. Simply translating a word literally from one language into another—with all the inadequacies of that approach—is not a reliable method for obtaining the kind of information we're looking for. Words, after all, never stand on their own; they never exist in a vacuum. They are always used in a certain context. Anthropologists are not so much interested in translating other people's terms and concepts as in translating other people's ideas, other images, and other ways of thinking. It's "cultural translation" that interests us.

*W*hen Boubakar and I discussed the difference between gaara and jingar, the meaning of jingar proved relatively simple to explain. Jingar—which is used both as a verb (to pray) and as a noun (prayer)—is the Songhay term for the ritual prayer that the second pillar of Islam requires Muslims to perform daily.

No other religious duty is prescribed by the Qur'an as often as the ritual prayers known as salât, and it is the duty to pray five times a day that encroaches more than any other upon the lives of observant Muslims. In Djenné, just as everywhere in the Islamic world, daily life is regulated by the times of prayer. Five times a day, worshippers perform the prescribed combination of bodily movements and formulaic recitations that together comprise the ritual prayer. Facing in the direction of Mecca, they repeat-

The main entrance to the mosque, after the Friday prayer.

d, kneel, and prostrate themselves, uttering at prescribed moments such phrases as "God is great" and reciting the first sura of the Qur'an and the profession of faith. The residents of Djenné carry out this religious duty after reaching a certain age. Some are more strict and zealous than others—I was frequently told that the first prayer of the day, performed between the first light of dawn and sunrise, requires the greatest strength of will—but by performing salât they assert their identity as Muslims.

While jingar is used only in the context of salât, gaara is used—as Boubakar pointed out—for all blessings. As an example he gave the customary blessing recited before retiring at night: "May God let you see the morrow." As Boubakar explained, "When one asks God for something, for His help, such entreaties are called gaara."

Gaara in which God is called upon to help and care for the faithful are ubiquitous in the daily life of Djenné. God is invoked constantly: "May God preserve us," "May God protect you on your journey," "May God let us see the morrow," "May God give us strength," "May God accept your alms," "May God make things easy for you," "May God grant you and us peace." These and many other formulas are uttered everywhere, every day, by everyone.

Reciting gaara is also a task of the marabouts. Just as the thirteenth-century Islamic scholars who assembled in Djenné to witness the conversion of the ruler Konboro prayed to God to bring prosperity to the city, present-day marabouts still recite gaara in which they entreat God to bless Djenné and its residents. Long series of gaara are recited on religious feast days in particular.

For all those in trouble, may God help them.
From the evil that awaits us in the coming year, may God protect us.
If the good fortune of this year comes from the north, may God grant it to us.
If it comes from the south, may God grant it to us.
From whichever direction it comes, may God grant it to us.
If it comes in the night, may God grant it to us.
If it comes in the daytime, may God grant it to us.
If it comes in the river, may God grant it to us.
If it comes from the left, may God grant it to us.
If it comes from the right, may God grant it to us.
From the evil of the coming year, may God protect us.
If it comes in the night, may God protect us.
If it comes in the daytime, may God protect us.
If it comes from the north, may God protect us.
If it comes from the south, may God protect us.
If it comes from the east, may God protect us.

If it comes from the west, may God protect us.
If it comes from the left, may God protect us.
If it comes from the right, may God protect us.
For all those who have problems, may God solve them.
To those having trouble conceiving, may God give them children.
To those men having trouble finding a spouse, may God give them a wife.
To those women having trouble finding a spouse, may God give them a husband.
To those with money problems, may God give them money.
To those having trouble learning, may God give them knowledge.
To those with health problems, may God cure them.
And those with problems and worries in this world and the next, may God help them.
These are the gaara that the elders have asked us to recite.
May God bless our master Muhammad and the family of our master Muhammad
and grant them peace.

It was with this series of gaara that Moussa Tanapo began to close the 1:00 AM gathering held to honor Muhammad's birthday. For nearly four hours, dozens of men—including marabouts, their advanced pupils, and several elders—had sung the Prophet's praises. Because of the special importance of the occasion, the gathering had lasted much longer than those of the previous evenings. The conclusion followed the same pattern, however: before all those present recited the first sura of the Qur'an three times by way of closing, a marabout or one of the older men in attendance recited a long series of gaara. Some of the marabouts, such as Tanapo, were known to be good at this, and so were often called upon to do it. A certain amount of skill is required to recite a number of gaara quickly and melodiously. I once heard an old man—whose advanced age had earned him the honor of reciting a number of gaara at the end of a gathering—stammer out the same line three times in a row, and the audience had laughed.

Sometimes a marabout went too far. One evening, after the poems had been recited in unison, a few short solos were sung in praise of the Prophet. Before the young singer had even reached the end of his song, however, I noticed that Ahmadou Traoré was muttering softly to himself. He had already begun the concluding series of gaara. Without missing a beat, he continued the blessings in a somewhat louder voice as soon as the young man finished his song. For nearly fifteen minutes Traoré continued to recite his gaara, undisturbed by the members of the audience who had meanwhile started to chat. While making our way home around midnight, I heard a number of men—including several marabouts who were walking behind us—having a rather heated conversation. I asked Boubakar what they were talking about, and he told me they were complaining about the number of gaara Traoré had recited that evening. They thought it had taken much too long. Tired from reading, all they wanted to do was go home.

Chapter Four

Marabouts recite gaara at other important religious meetings as well. The daily readings from the Qur'an during Ramadan and the special prayers said on the two major Islamic feast days—the end of Ramadan and the Festival of Sacrifice—are concluded with gaara in which God's blessing for the entire population of Djenné is invoked.

But the critical times in a person's life, moments when an individual passes from one phase of life to the next, are also accompanied by gaara.

May God grant him a long life.
May God make his mother's milk strong.
May God give him the strength to reinforce our ranks.
May God let him live as a Muslim.
May God grant him happiness if he continues to live in Djenné, and may He grant him happiness if he goes to live elsewhere.
May God let us witness their marriage.
May God let us witness the naming of their children.
May God let us witness the circumcision of their children.
May God grant them a good marriage.
May God allow the man to provide for his family and the woman to give birth to many children.
May God grant them a long and healthy life.
May God let them live together in harmony.
May God have mercy on him.
May God forgive him.
May God lay him to rest in a wide grave.
May God not question him too much.
May God send him a compassionate angel.
May God grant him eternal life in paradise.

Life in Djenné plays itself out among these four kinds of gaara, at least if one lives long enough to be given a name, to be circumcised, and to marry. Gaara like these mark the transitions between the various stages of human existence. In theory everyone is entitled to utter such congratulatory or consolatory blessings, but in practice marabouts are the ones who usually recite gaara on the occasions that call for them: when a child's name is proclaimed, seven days after its birth; when circumcised boys leave the house where they have been secluded for two weeks after their circumcision; when a marriage has been solemnized in the presence of family members of both the bride and the groom; when the mourners return to the house of the deceased after the burial.

It is not only gaara in which God's name is invoked. In Djenné, as in the whole of the Islamic world, the expression *inshallah* ("God willing") is heard constantly. Many wishes for future happiness or greater prosperity end with inshallah. As it says in the Qur'an: "And do not say of anything: 'I shall do this tomorrow' unless you add: 'If God wills'" (18:23–24). The use of inshallah resembles the recitation of gaara. Something is requested of God, and He may grant the request. Boubakar once told me the story of the Majuj (in the Old Testament they are called the Magog), which illustrates this point.

Behind the known world, on the other side of a barrier of rock and boulders, live the Majuj, a people who seek to reach the other side by eating the stones that block their way. Every day they eat so many stones that only a small bit of the barrier remains, after which they withdraw to rest from their labors. The next day, however, they always find that the remaining rocks have grown back to their original size, so that they must start all over again. This will go on and on, until such day as a Majuj woman bears a son who shall be named Inshallah. When Inshallah is old enough, he will go with his father to eat stones, and at the end of the day, when only a small amount remains, the father will call to his son: "We're going home now, Inshallah, tomorrow we'll reach the other side." The next day the rocks will not have grown back to their original size, and on that day the Majuj will reach the other side. Nothing will hold them back this time. Only when one of these stone-eating people invokes God, calling upon Him to ensure the prosperity of their undertaking, will they finally reach their goal. They will eat up the very last rock, and the day this happens will coincide with the end of time.

Other expressions—likewise derived from the Qur'an—such as *bismillah* (in the name of God) and *alhamdulillah* (praise be to God) are heard even more frequently than inshallah in daily communication. At the beginning of a meal or a conversation, when inviting people into one's home or handing them something—in any of these situations and a host of others—one recites the opening words of the Qur'an: "In the name of God." Thus, one invokes God to bless what one is about to do. And just as bismillah is uttered at the beginning, alhamdulillah is uttered at the end. This formula can also be used to express surprise or agreement. *Yer Koy saabu*, the Songhay equivalent of alhamdulillah, serves the same purpose. Frequently used as an interjection, it is continually heard in the series of questions and answers that form salutations: "How are you this morning?" "I am well, God be praised." "How did you sleep last night?" "I slept well, God be praised." "How are the members of your family?" "They are well, God be praised." Whenever people meet, God's name is praised.

*D*uring one of our visits to Abdoulaye Touré, the conversation turned to the subject of death and the afterlife. The marabout told us that the souls of the virtuous remain in heaven while awaiting Judgment Day, whereas those of unbelievers are locked in the "prison" below the seventh

strate that the time of one's death is predetermined and no
e it, Touré told the story of "the boy and the angel of death."
n a time Azrail, the angel of death, was visiting the prophet
Solomon. The two of them were talking, and a boy was sitting with them.
Solomon glanced at the boy and thought he looked terrified. He was right,
because no sooner had Azrail left than the boy told him how frightened he
had been of the visitor. He asked Solomon—to whom God had given
power over the wind—to convey him immediately to China. Solomon
honored his request and ordered the wind to whisk the boy off to China.
Later that same day, the angel Azrail returned to Solomon. "When you
were here this morning, why did you look at that boy the way you did?"
Solomon asked the angel. Azrail told him how surprised he had been to
find the boy there, because in the dossier he had received on the boy, it had
been recorded that he would die that day in China. The prophet then told
the angel that the boy had asked to be taken to China and that he had
ordered the wind to do so. When the boy's appointed hour of death had
come, Azrail replied, he had gone to China to take the boy's life.

"Everything that happens in the world and to its people, the children
of Adam, is written," said Touré. The story of the boy and Azrail clearly
illustrates this. The time of one's death and everything else in life is preordained—even the conversation Boubakar and I were having with him at
that moment. It was possible, the marabout said, that I wanted to ask
some more questions, but if those questions were not "written," I would
find that this was not the time to ask them.

Everything is already written down. Long before creation God
recorded everything that will happen in the world on the "well-preserved
tablet" (al-lawh al-mahfuz, in Arabic). If it is recorded that a person will die
in a certain place, that is where he will die. If it is recorded that a person's
destiny will be fulfilled in a certain place, that person will find himself in
that particular place on the predetermined day.

"For example," Touré aptly explained, "if it is written that the destiny
of a man from Djenné will be fulfilled in Holland, that is where he will
find his fortune. This can happen in one of two ways. The first possibility is
that he will meet a man from Holland here in Djenné. Neither knows he
will meet the other, but on the preordained day, the man from Djenné will
meet the visitor from Holland and through him find his fortune, God having instructed His angels to bring about their meeting. The second possibility is that, as the preordained day approaches, the man from Djenné will
suddenly have the opportunity to travel to Holland, where he will find his
fortune, even though he had no inkling that this would happen. In this way
all the food you eat and all the water you drink is distributed over various
places. If it is written that you will eat for the last time on a certain day and

in a certain place, you will be unable to eat anything there after that time. You will undertake a journey, and there's nothing you can do to avoid it."

"But if the course of one's life is preordained, why do people call on marabouts for help?" we asked Touré.

"All things have a cause," the marabout began, "but things are of three kinds." And he explained this as follows: first, there are things that simply happen to you, and you are powerless to prevent them; second, there are things that can be achieved, but you must ask for them by reciting gaara; and third, there are things that can be obtained by giving alms (*saraa*).

"Everything has already been written," the marabout continued, "but God has said even more. He says in the Qur'an: 'Call upon Me and I shall answer you,' which shows that if only we ask, we will be given things and protected from harm. It is as the Prophet said: 'Gaara are the weapons of the believer.' They can be used for protection."

Not long after this talk, Boubakar and I were sitting at my desk, working up the notes I'd taken during this conversation. We went over what the marabout had told us. When we arrived at the Prophet's pronouncement that gaara were the weapons of the faithful, Boubakar was prompted to say, "Everyone, rich or poor, can invoke God by reciting gaara. But marabouts are usually able to follow the 'way of God' better than others. They are the ones who read His Book every day and recite His Word. They are the ones who teach God's Word, and are therefore in the best position to intercede with God on another's behalf. They can petition God for other people. After all, as God said: 'Learn to know me before serving me.'"

Several days later, when I reminded Boubakar of the words he had quoted to show that marabouts knew best how to intercede with God, he pointed out, yet again, that everybody can invoke God's name. Anyone can recite gaara, and God listens to everyone.

"But," he emphasized this time, "some of God's names and words from the Qur'an are heard sooner than others, and when they are used in a gaara, they ensure a quicker result." And he reminded me, by way of example, that Abdoulaye Touré had told us that the Qur'an contained various words that could be incorporated in headache remedies.

There were many such words in the Qur'an, Boubakar explained. Everything you need—whether to cure an illness or solve a problem—can be found in the great Qur'an. In His Book, God revealed everything to His Prophet. But people don't always know which passage they need; they haven't all studied "on that level." The people who know these important passages are the marabouts. The words used to invoke God's name—the ones heard the quickest—are secret. It is the marabouts who know where to find these words in the Qur'an. They are the ones who know how to address petitionary prayers to God.

Sidi Nientao (ca. 1925–1991), muezzin of the mosque of Djenné

Chapter 5

The Future Holds Secrets

*A*nthropological fieldwork can be frustrating at times, and working in Djenné was no exception. Some of the people I interviewed gave only the vaguest of answers; others I wanted to speak to were never at home or—even worse—pretended not to be. Sometimes the information I gleaned at interviews was completely contradictory, and at times our talks were interrupted at a crucial moment by the arrival of another person. There were important events I missed because I didn't hear about them in time, and incidents I witnessed but didn't understand. My confidence in the success of my research was sometimes shaken, but luckily I had Boubakar. When a marabout had been rather uncommunicative and I couldn't hide my disappointment, Boubakar would try to lift my spirits by quoting a Songhay proverb: "The child who keeps to himself will be grown up one day." It was not good to ask too much, he told me at such times. It was better to be patient and stay calm; modesty was the best policy. This would produce results in the end; haste was never good. "The bird builds its nest bit by bit," he added for good measure.

Although Boubakar's words of wisdom cheered me up, and his help and assistance kept me going when my fieldwork seemed to reach a dead end, *he* was sometimes the reason my plans went awry. Occasionally he arrived an hour or two late, because he had overslept or needed to take care of some urgent business. At other times he made no effort to hide the fact that he wasn't in the mood for our talk with a marabout, and our visit was ruined by the resulting tension.

Now and then Boubakar was preoccupied with something that distracted him from my research: his girlfriend, for example, was for a while a great source of worry. She had gone to live in a village about thirty kilometers north of Djenné to help keep house for a distant relative, but had stayed away much longer than planned. Boubakar had expected her back a long time ago, and wondered whether she was all right. Sometimes he was so lost in thought that my fieldwork was relegated to the sidelines. And yet Boubakar's personal problems also resulted in a number of interesting encounters.

One day Boubakar mentioned to Brahima Coulibaly, who could read the turaabu, that he had a problem. Coulibaly told him to come around that evening, and I went along. We sat down in the vestibule of Coulibaly's house, and Boubakar explained his problem: his girlfriend had been away for too long, and he kept wondering when she would come home. Coulibaly handed Boubakar a reed pen, which he held to his mouth for several seconds before gently spitting on the nib. He gave the pen back to Coulibaly, who spit on it, dipped it in ink, and started to make little marks on a board smeared with washed-off ink. Moving his hand swiftly up and down, he soon filled the upper left-hand corner of the board with 16 rows, more or less equal in length, of short, curly strokes. Holding the board in the light of the kerosene lamp, Coulibaly began— row by row, from right to left—to cross out the vertical strokes, two at a time. He kept going until only one or two strokes were left at the end of every row, and after four rows, he set the remaining strokes apart. Coulibaly performed this operation four times, until the original 16 rows had been reduced to four tetragrams, each consisting of four rows of one or two strokes. This pattern was to be the basis for another 12 tetragrams, but before Coulibaly had made the calculations that enabled him to fill in all 16 "houses" of the turaabu, he put his client's mind at rest. He turned to Boubakar and informed him that the situation was favorable: his girlfriend was longing to return to Djenné.

When he had finished the entire turaabu, Coulibaly reiterated that Boubakar had nothing to worry about, since his girlfriend wanted to come home. She thought about him even more than he thought about her. Their love would never die. She hadn't come home yet simply because the person she was staying with wouldn't let her go.

Relieved by the reassurance of his girlfriend's love, Boubakar asked Coulibaly another question: if he were to visit his girlfriend in the village where she was staying, would she return with him to Djenné or would there be a problem?

From a small pile of books and manuscripts lying in the corner of the vestibule, Coulibaly took a leather folder full of unbound papers, leafed through them for a minute, removed a couple of sheets, and set them aside. Then he took out his prayer beads (*tasbiya*) and handed them to Boubakar. As he had done with the pen, Boubakar held the beads to his

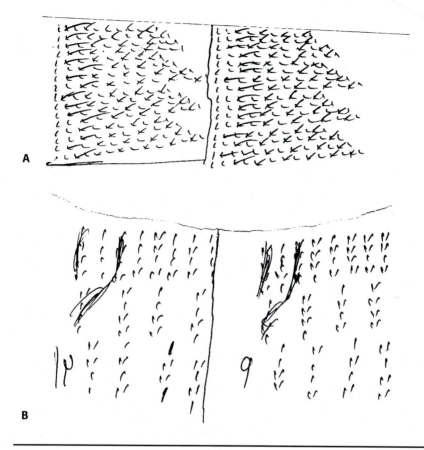

Figure 5.1 Two views (left and right) of the table of the turaabu written in ballpoint pen on paper.

(A) At the top are the 16 rows of short strokes from which the figures in the table are derived. In each row these strokes are crossed out—from right to left, two at a time—until only one or two remain. These binary signs form (in groups of four lines, from top to bottom) the figures that will appear in the first four "houses" of the table (in the upper row, from right to left). They serve as the basis of transpositions (of horizontal lines into vertical columns) and calculations (adding up two figures to yield a subsequent figure) that determine how the other 12 "houses" are to be filled in.

(B) In each table, the figures in three houses—the sixth ("the house of the sick"), the eighth ("the house of death"), and the twelfth ("the house of enemies")—have been crossed out. Such deletions serve to keep the outcome of the divination secret, "in case someone who knows the turaabu happens to glance at it." I do not know the meaning of the two Arabic numerals (12 beside the left table and 9 beside the table on the right).

mouth for a few seconds, spit on them gently, and handed them back to Coulibaly, who spit on them as well, then laid them on the mat, mumbled something, and closed his eyes. Coulibaly proceeded to circle his head with his index finger three times, and then, without looking, picked up the string by one bead, which he grasped between his thumb and index finger. Opening his eyes, he started with this bead and counted off the rest until he came to the tassel. Finally, he picked up the papers he had laid aside, scanned them until he found the right place, and read silently to himself for a moment. Again addressing Boubakar, he announced that this result was also favorable: his girlfriend would come back to Djenné and there would be no problem, but it would help if he were to go and fetch her, because then she would come home immediately.

When we asked Coulibaly about the paper he'd consulted, he told us that the following passage was written next to the number that corresponded to the number of beads he'd counted off: "He who is looking for a woman to marry will find her, and there will be no problem. If one asks oneself whether a traveler will return soon, the answer is that there is no problem: he will return quickly and in good health. If a sick man asks whether he will be cured, the answer is that there is no problem: he will get better."

Completely reassured by Coulibaly's prediction, Boubakar handed him a 50-franc coin: a small gift "for good luck." When we were outside again, Boubakar said that it was customary to give something, even if only a token amount, for such a consult, to bring "good luck" and to guarantee and expedite a successful outcome. "There are people who give 100 francs for this kind of work, and those who give 500," he explained. "It depends on what you can afford."

Back home I asked Boubakar exactly what he had been doing when he held the pen Coulibaly had used to consult the turaabu. He told me he had recited to himself the following words: "O God, Knower of the Invisible and the Visible. O God, I beseech you to reveal by this means whether my girlfriend will return soon. O God, Almighty, All-Wise." Boubakar explained that "by this means" referred to the turaabu, and he added: "Each of us asks in his own way." In any case, this was his way of posing the question he hoped to see answered in the turaabu, because, as it says in the Qur'an, God is "the Knower of the Invisible and the Visible."

$\mathcal{A}$bout a week after our visit to Brahima Coulibaly, Boubakar and I were having a Nescafé at André's coffeehouse on the market square.

Inside the stuffy room, where a kettle of water simmered on a smoky fire all day long, André was waiting on a customer who had ordered a slice of French bread with mayonnaise along with his coffee. It was more pleasant outside, at least until the sun rose so high that there was no longer a strip of shadow in front of the shops and warehouses. André, a Dogon and one of the few Christians in town, had previously worked at the Hotel-Campement, but some time ago he had set up his own business, running this simple café in an old warehouse. Now and then Boubakar and I went there for a cup of coffee in the middle of the morning, and sat for a while on the wooden bench that André always carried outside for us. It was one of my favorite places in Djenné.

The entrance to the daily market was a few meters to our left. At the gate that opened onto the arcaded square where the market women sold their wares, young girls selling rice and millet cakes praised their goods in high-pitched voices. On the other side of the square, which was quiet and abandoned after the bustle of the Monday market, the morning sun cast its rays on the monumental east façade of the mosque. At this hour of the day the mud had a yellowish color. As always, the Great Mosque was an impressive sight: the three massive towers, the middle and largest one containing the prayer niche; the pilasters, which had been applied to the wall between the towers; the smaller, square, corner towers, ending in pinnacles; and the rows of palm-wood sticks jutting out of the wall. It was not only this façade but the entire building that was splendid. Like a statue on a pedestal, it stood there, elevated above the square, on a broad plateau: the crowning glory of this mud town. From my very first morning in Djenné—when I had hastened to the market square to see the mosque that I knew from so many pictures—I had been fascinated by the most beautiful building in West Africa, which the American architectural historian Jean-Louis Bourgeois has described as "mud at its most majestic."

While women and girls carrying bowls and baskets on their heads made their way to the market, we drank our coffee and discussed the subject troubling Boubakar the most—his girlfriend's absence—and this led to a discussion of our last visit to Baber Kontao.

The day after Boubakar had asked Brahima Coulibaly to consult the turaabu for him, Boubakar had suggested we visit Baber Kontao. Kontao, a marabout, was often away, visiting towns such as Bamako, Mopti, Segou, and the surrounding villages, where he had been invited—or had invited himself—to put his knowledge of maraboutage to good use. When he was in town, we dropped in on him occasionally to say hello. At our last meeting, Boubakar had brought up the subject of his absent girlfriend and asked Kontao for his advice.

The Great Mosque of Djenné (built in 1907) dominates the market square like a statue on a pedestal.

Using a ballpoint pen, Kontao had drawn the vertical strokes of the turaabu on a sheet of writing paper and filled in the various "houses." After examining the results, he put Boubakar's mind at rest. There was no need for him to worry. It would not be long before his girlfriend returned to Djenné. But if he wanted to hasten this happy event, Boubakar would have to give saraa. Kontao went to fetch some papers, and after consulting them, he told Boubakar that he should give a red goat and a kola nut shaped like a horse's head. Boubakar was shocked. A goat was far too expensive. Again Kontao consulted his papers, and said that if a red goat was too expensive, a red chicken would do. Boubakar agreed to this. As usual, the marabout did not say to whom the saraa should be given. It was up to the client to decide which needy person would benefit from his alms. God would reward him for his good deed.

That same afternoon Boubakar went to a trader in kola nuts and spent a long time looking for one in the shape of a horse's head. He didn't buy the red chicken, though, because he would have had to wait several days for the Monday market, and it was best to deal with such matters as quickly as possible. Fortunately, when a prescribed saraa is difficult to obtain, money will also suffice.

Several hours after Baber Kontao had told him what to do to hasten his girlfriend's return, Boubakar gave "Grandma Ata" a kola nut shaped like a horse's head and 300 francs—the price of a red chicken. "Please accept my saraa," he said to Ata as he handed her these things, and the old woman replied, "May God grant your wish." Since there is no need to reveal the exact nature of the wish, neither the giver nor the receiver mentioned it.

Sitting on the bench outside André's coffeehouse, we went over the matter of Boubakar's absent girlfriend another time. Even though the outcome of the turaabu had again been favorable, Boubakar was still preoccupied with the whole affair. This time he proposed doing what Brahima Coulibaly had suggested: going in person to fetch his girlfriend.

A short while later we were presented with an opportunity to put this plan into action. We were offered a ride by someone going to Mopti, who would let us out at the village where Boubakar's girlfriend was staying and pick us up again in the afternoon. Encouraged by the fact that Brahima Coulibaly had not anticipated any problems, we left town in the morning, only to come back empty-handed at the end of the day, having been fobbed off with the feeble excuse that the "aunt" would send her guest home at the end of the week.

"The marabouts failed to predict this," I remarked to Boubakar.

He couldn't help laughing. "That's for sure, they were way off the mark." One day he would go and tell them so.

Two days later Boubakar reported that he'd gone to see Baber Kontao, who hadn't been at home. Boubakar had, however, told Coulibaly about our useless journey. The marabout pointed out that the turaabu had correctly revealed that Boubakar's girlfriend had wanted to leave, but had been prevented from doing so by her hostess. But he didn't mention his second prediction—based on prayer-bead divination—that everything would go smoothly.

A few days later Boubakar also spoke to Baber Kontao about our visit to his girlfriend. He didn't come right out and tell him to his face that his predictions—and those of the other marabout he had consulted—had been incorrect, but he did hint at it. Kontao didn't comment. Boubakar asked him what he should do, now that the plan to bring his girlfriend back to Djenné had failed. Was it advisable to examine the matter again, or should he simply bide his time? Once more the marabout consulted the turaabu. This time the two outcomes pointed to two different possibilities: the first result predicted she wouldn't come; the second predicted she would. But the second result, which was the "stronger" of the two, predicted that between 2:00 and 4:00 PM the following day, Boubakar's girlfriend would come to Djenné with her "aunt," who would summon Boubakar and tell him that if he wanted to marry his girlfriend, he would have to come up with the bride-price. Boubakar was horrified by this prediction, and told Kontao angrily that if the woman said that to him, he would tell her in no uncertain terms how things stood. After all, he and his girlfriend had not met in *her* house, and anyway, she was not the girl's mother. If this "aunt" made things difficult for him, he would break up with the girl. The marabout urged him to stay calm and not to act hastily, reminding him that the "aunt" and not his girlfriend had been responsible for her long absence.

When the next afternoon had come and gone with no news of his girlfriend's arrival, Boubakar went back to see Kontao and confronted him with the fact that she still hadn't returned. "Ah, but at least they've packed their bags," the marabout had replied.

This all goes to show, Boubakar concluded, that it could be dangerous to pay frequent visits to a marabout and ask him to consult the turaabu. He might tell you something that wasn't true, and you might act on it anyway, and then things would turn out badly. Boubakar had gotten all worked up for nothing. Since the marabouts had mistakenly assured him that his girlfriend would soon return to Djenné, Boubakar had lost faith in their pronouncements. It would be better, he said, to consult them only in the case of extremely serious matters, but even then, you had to beware. "Often their predictions are simply not true," Boubakar said. "But nobody can know everything. Nobody but God."

*T*uraabu is derived from the Arabic word *turab*, which means dust, earth, or sand. The patterns upon which the diviner bases his conclusions—nowadays recorded with pen and ink on a writing board, or with a ballpoint pen on paper—were originally written with a finger in the sand. The origin of this geomantic technique can be traced to a revelation to the prophet Idris (Enoch). When we asked marabouts in Djenné about this, they claimed that knowledge of the turaabu had been given to Idris by the angel Jibril (Gabriel).

In the early 1940s the French researcher Bernard Maupoil (1943) recorded in Bas-Dahomey, the southern part of present-day Benin, the following version of this story. Once upon a time Idris asked God to give him a livelihood that required little work. Seated in the inner courtyard of his house, Idris waited patiently for God to honor his request. One day, while running his fingers through the sand, a man appeared and asked Idris what he was doing.

"I'm amusing myself by playing with this sand," he answered.

"No," the stranger countered, "you're not amusing yourself. You're engaging in very serious work."

That apparition was the angel Jibril, who had come to reveal to Idris what in Arabic is called *khatt al-raml*, writing in the sand.

Louis Brenner (1985a), the American historian and expert on Islam in West Africa, also quotes this story in one of his articles, in which he observes that, while the story legitimizes diviners' activities by basing them on God's revelation to one of His prophets, at the same time it lends their practices a certain ambiguity. Knowledge of "writing in the sand" was indeed revealed to man, but only as an easy way to make a living. According to Brenner, "from an orthodox standpoint, divination is in the margin of Islam."

In the writings of classical Islamic scholars, divination is viewed as a dubious and objectionable practice. The fourteenth-century North African historian Ibn Khaldun (1967) stated that the knowledge of the supernatural that is sought through astrology and geomancy is "meaningless in both theory and practice," because, he added, quoting a line that occurs in various places in the Qur'an, "God knows and you do not know."

Revealing secret matters is also not without risk. "You must beware of making predictions," a young marabout once told us. "The turaabu can reveal a person's secret intentions, but people do not always act on their intentions. Suppose you hear something bad about someone and stop being friends with him, even though he might have changed his mistaken ways if only you had continued your friendship. You run the risk of ruining a friendship for no good reason. The moment you hear something bad about a person, you start to behave differently toward him. Only God knows the future. All you need to do is put your trust in Him."

*O*n a corner of the Monday market I occasionally witnessed the cowrie-shell divination known throughout West Africa. The diviner throws down a dozen cowrie shells—whose rounded tops have been ground away, so that they can lie on either side—and interprets their patterns to find the answer to his client's question. Various people told me that this practice was incompatible with Islam.

When we asked the marabout Abdoulaye Touré why "seeing the cowries," as it is called, was forbidden by the Islamic religion, he said that all methods of divination—including that of cowrie shells—were to be condemned. Knowledge of the future is reserved for God alone. "One can consult the turaabu," he said, "and one can use prayer beads or see certain things in dreams. These are all ways of predicting the future, but they are all incompatible with our religion. Only God knows what the future holds in store."

But weren't marabouts trying to do just that—predict the future—when people came to them for help? If the religion condemned divination, shouldn't marabouts condemn it as well?

"People do what is frowned upon," was his short but firm reply. "Still," Touré added by way of qualification, "just because a marabout examines a client's 'situation' doesn't mean he tells him everything. For example, a marabout can examine his client's destiny with regard to 'finding' money; perhaps he tells him what he must do to 'find' money but says nothing about the other things he has seen. A marabout does not necessarily reveal everything to his client."

On an earlier occasion Touré had explained how marabouts foretell their clients' future. To determine a person's destiny, only two things are necessary: the person's name and that of his or her mother. If the mother's name is unknown, the name of Hawwa (Eve) will suffice, since she is the mother of us all. The marabout begins by calculating the numerical value of these two names, therefore knowledge of numerology is essential. Each letter of the Arabic alphabet has a certain value. The numbers from 1 to 10, multiples of 10, multiples of 100, and the number 1,000 are each assigned to one of the 28 letters of the alphabet. The numerical value of a word is thus the sum of the values of its individual letters. To determine a man's lot in life, one must add the numerical value of his name to that of his mother's and divide the result by 12. The resulting number refers to one of the 12 *buruj*, the signs of the zodiac. When this is known, the marabout can consult a book to predict his client's future.

Touré had progressed this far in his explanation when he suddenly went off on a tangent. I made a few cautious attempts to get our conversation back on track, but to no avail. The marabout was obviously reluctant to reveal more.

On another occasion I had high hopes of learning more about a person's destiny, the signs of the zodiac, and, by extension, divination in general—particularly since the subject had crept unobtrusively into our conversation. Once again, however, my eagerness for more precise knowledge was not to be rewarded.

It was New Year's Day 1991. Apart from the New Year's messages broadcast on the radio by the president and several lesser politicians, to which Boubakar and I had listened early in the morning, there was nothing to suggest that this was the first day of the new year: life went on as usual. We decided to pay a visit to Abdoulaye Touré.

During the informal conversation following the customary exchange of greetings and preceding my prepared questions, Boubakar suggested that I wish the marabout a "Happy New Year." Somewhat surprised, I apologized and said that I had thought that the first day of the Christian calendar would have meant little to the people of Djenné. Boubakar translated this for the marabout, who replied, "Naturally it means something to us as well."

There are two eras, Touré explained, based on the sun and the moon. When a child is born, both eras are taken into account: the date according to the Muslim era, based on moon years, and the date by Christian reckoning, based on sun years. Both can be recorded as one's date of birth. The most important thing, however, is not a person's date of birth but the star under which he or she is born. In determining a person's buruj, the date of birth is of no use. This method is too imprecise and can lead to incorrect results. The day can be "good," but the hour "bad," and it is the hour of birth that influences one's lot in life. Even twins do not share the same fate. A much more accurate method of determining a person's buruj, Touré explained, is through calculations based on the person's name and that of his or her mother, because, he added, one can never be certain about the identity of the father.

The marabout picked up a booklet that lay next to him on the mat. It was a small bilingual diary, printed in Morocco, for the year 1991. Written next to the months and days (in French) of the Christian year were the Arabic months and days of the Islamic year 1411–1412. He turned over a couple of pages and pointed to the word *dalu*. "Bucket," translated

Boubakar. Touré reached for the bulging briefcase he always had with him, took out a file folder, and undid the cord wrapped around it. He rifled through the file, took out a booklet, and began to leaf through it. I could see sketches of the signs of the zodiac, including those of Gemini and Scorpio. When Touré had found the dalu, he showed us a picture of a man holding a bucket on a rope: Aquarius.

What did it mean if someone was born under this star? I asked. What did the words next to this sign mean? My questions went unanswered. There was no need for me to understand it, Touré replied. I shouldn't even try to comprehend such a difficult subject. Not only was it time-consuming, but not everyone was capable of acquiring such knowledge. One could spend three years just learning the basics. It had taken him two years, he told us, and then he quickly steered the conversation in another direction.

*B*oubakar had once owned a booklet that could be used to "examine a person's situation." It was called *Qur'atu 'l-anbiyâ'*. He couldn't remember what he'd done with it, though, so we resolved to go in search of a copy. We asked a couple of booksellers in town, who didn't have it in stock but promised to look for it the next time they went to buy books in Mopti or Bamako. In the end we found a second-hand copy at the market in Mopti. It was a slender volume of 16 pages.

Qur'atu 'l-anbiyâ' might be translated as one's destiny according to the prophets. The first page features a table divided into 32 squares, each containing the name of a prophet, somewhat analogous to the "houses" of the turaabu. The text in the square in the upper right-hand corner reads "the lot (*sahm*) of Adam, peace be with him," while the text in the square in the lower left-hand corner reads "the lot of Muhammad, may peace and God's blessings be upon him." The other 30 squares contain the names of such prophets as Noah, Abraham, Joseph, Solomon, Moses, Job, Jesus, and Daniel, followed by "peace be with him."

Boubakar had occasionally consulted the *Qur'atu 'l-anbiyâ'* with regard to his own problems. He was certain that there were marabouts in Djenné who owned this book and used it to examine their own and their clients' "situation." He explained how it was done.

"If you have a question you need answered, if you're in doubt about something, if you feel out of sorts or fearful, then you say to yourself, in your mind and in your heart, 'I don't know what's wrong with me, may God reveal it to me' or 'How will my upcoming journey go, may God reveal it to me.' Or perhaps you have a question about your health, or you're looking for a wife, or you need money. There are a million things you could ask. We all have our own problems, and you can consult the book about each and every one of them. You formulate your question, close your eyes, and recite the al-Fatiha sura three times while circling your head with your right index finger. Without looking, you put this finger on the table. Next to the name of the prophet in whose house your finger landed you'll find—further on in the book—the answer to your question: an answer such as 'You shouldn't waste your time with such matters. It's not worth the trouble. You won't find the answer' or 'Your undertaking will succeed. You must get started right away' or 'There's a woman who will approach you with her plan and her deceitful ways. Don't trust her. Ask God to protect you from this evil.'"

I asked Boubakar to translate some of the answers given in the book, and we spent a couple of afternoons doing this. What took the most time was tracking down the passages quoted from the Qur'an. As usual, Boubakar never translated words from the Holy Book. We made use of my bilingual copy of the Qur'an, in which he searched for the verse in question. This entailed much leafing back and forth, especially when he didn't know exactly where to look. Sometimes we failed to find the passage we were looking for, even after searching long and hard. Boubakar was no *hafiz*, he would emphasize at such times. Unlike some people in Djenné, he did not know the whole Qur'an by heart. Still, I had to find the Dutch translation before we could discuss the quotation.

The problem with translating passages from the Qur'an—which Muslims consider "the uncreated word of God" and therefore untranslatable—was summed up by Boubakar as follows: "It contains things that man does not know; it contains things that man does not understand. You may have a great deal of knowledge, but you can't explain everything. Even a little word like *bi*, the very first word in the Qur'an, can be translated in an infinite number of ways. That's why marabouts translate passages from the Qur'an only in the broadest of terms."

For example, the Qur'anic passage referred to in "the lot of Yusuf (Joseph)" reads as follows: "He said: 'Rather, your souls have tempted you to some act. O seemly patience! It may be that God will bring them all back to me; He is All-Knowing, All-Wise'" (12:83). Therefore, "he whose destiny this is" is advised to keep his "secret" so that his undertaking will be successful. He should not trust others, because they will try to mislead him. But just as Joseph was delivered from the hands of his brothers, he will be spared misfortune by the power of God and His Prophet.

If the finger of the person consulting the *Qurʿatu 'l-anbiyâ'* lands on "the lot of Danyal (Daniel)," this is a sign of good luck and strength in all circumstances, though here, too, one has to beware of enemies, one of whom is particularly persistent and bent on ruining the "owner of this lot" and "attacking him with his tongue." One should ask for God's help and have faith in Him. After all, as God, the most Exalted, said: "Whoso places his trust in God, God shall suffice him. God enforces what He commands. For all things God has set a measure" (65:3).

$\mathscr{H}$amidou Sanogo read out loud from the handwritten sheet of paper he was holding in his hand. After every few words of Arabic, he stopped to translate the passage into Songhay. "This is the year of the prophet Idris," he said. "It will be a good year."

It was early in the morning of *ashura*, the tenth day of the first month of the Islamic year 1407: September 15, 1986, according to the Christian calendar. Boubakar and I were sitting in the vestibule of Hamidou Sanogo's house, together with about twenty older men and women. Many of those present were Sanogo's relatives or neighbors. We had all come to hear the new year's tidings (*jiiri alkabaar*).

On the feast day of ashura, the gathering began with gaara and the recitation of the opening sura of the Qur'an. Sanogo started off with a number of gaara in Arabic, so that God might grant everyone "the good in this world and the good in the next world." He then invited the oldest man present to recite a number of gaara. The man said in Songhay, "May God let us all live to see the coming year. May God let us live to see the end of this year. Just as we have gathered together for this reading today, may we meet here in the same way for next year's reading. May God grant us this." Then all those present recited, as they did on numerous other occasions, the al-Fatiha sura three times, each led, as usual, by another of the oldest men present. While he uttered the words aloud, the others murmured softly, with their lower arms outstretched and palms held upward, the seven lines of the Qur'an's opening sura. After each closing *amin*, they wiped their hands over their faces. When al-Fatiha had been recited three times, the men shook each other's hands and exchanged new year's greetings. "May God let us all live to see the coming year. May God hear our prayers." The women, who were sitting on the other side of the vestibule, did the same.

After this, Hamidou Sanogo read the predictions for the coming year as they are written in the *jiiri-fita* (literally, year-leaves or year-sheets). "The year of the prophet Idris" would be a good year. The crops would be good. Work would yield results. Any journeys undertaken would go well. Many women would become pregnant and have healthy babies. Nothing bad would happen this year. But it was advisable not to go out on the streets around noon or at night, because if there were any problems with *djinns* this year, that is when they would occur. In the coming year, the men had to give five cowrie shells as alms (saraa), and the women four. The town chief had to give saraa consisting of a white robe, a white sheep, some milk, and a slave. He also had to write the following words 30 times on a piece of paper and bury it in the middle of town: *Yâ Hakîm, yâ Azîz, yâ Djabbâr, yâ Ahmad, yâ Samad* (O Wise, O Powerful, O Subjector, O Praiseworthy, O Eternal). All the other residents of the town were also advised to write these names of God on a piece of paper and bury it somewhere in their house, to protect themselves from evil djinns.

Nodding and grunting occasionally in approval, everyone listened to the predictions for the year 1407. When Hamidou Sanogo came to the end of the list, we all stood up. Once again, everyone exchanged the wish that God would let them live to see the coming year, and then filed outside, where several other neighbors were waiting to ask Sanogo what the coming year held in store. In a more informal way he would tell them— and everyone else who came to see him that day—what they might expect in the new year.

On the afternoon of ashura we paid another visit to Hamidou Sanogo. I still had a number of questions about the morning's reading. Sanogo reached for the jiiri-fita, remarking as he did so that they had been in the possession of his family for a long time.

We asked him to tell us what was written in the jiiri-fita. Sanogo began by explaining that there were seven kinds of years, each with its own character and each connected to a certain prophet. Whatever had occurred during the prophet's lifetime would occur again in the year that bore his name.

To determine what kind of year it was, you only had to know the day on which ashura fell. Sanogo perused the old, discolored, and well-thumbed pages, and read out the names of the prophets and the various years, one by one. If ashura fell, as it did this year, on a Monday, it was the year of the prophet Idris (Enoch); if ashura fell on a Tuesday, it was the year of Yaqub (Jacob); if it fell on a Wednesday, it was the year of Is'haq (Isaac); Thursday meant the year of Ibrahim (Abraham); Friday, Musa (Moses); Saturday, Isa (Jesus); and finally, if ashura fell on a Sunday, it was the year of Adam. The jiiri-fita described the characteristics of each year. It also specified which saraa should be given each year to ward off evil, and stipulated the names of God or passages from the Qur'an that had to be written down to accomplish this.

What about the cowrie shells and the slave that were supposed to be given as saraa in a year of Idris, we asked Sanogo. He explained that people now gave money instead of the cowrie shells used in the olden days: five francs for one cowrie. And instead of a slave, the town chief could give, say, a horse or a cow. Would the chief really give these alms, and would he actually write the required names on a piece of paper and bury it in the middle of town? Sanogo's reply was brief and to the point: he didn't know, and it was none of his business.

Boubakar had told me earlier that one could always go back to Sanogo and ask him to repeat the names of God needed to ward off evil. Because we were there anyway, Boubakar now took advantage of the opportunity to write down the names recorded in the jiiri-fita. While Sanogo read them out, Boubakar jotted them down on a sheet of paper I had torn out of my notebook.

On the way home I asked Boubakar whether he too would write the names of God 30 times on a piece of paper and bury it in his house. He replied that he would certainly think about it. It offered protection, after all. I don't know if he actually did it, since I never asked him and he never told me. But as far as almsgiving was concerned, when I asked Boubakar if he intended to give the saraa stipulated by Sanogo, his answer was unequivocal: he regularly gave saraa, he said, and assured me that the 25 francs the marabout had recommended would pose no problem.

A year later, on the morning of ashura of the Islamic year 1408, Sanogo read out the predictions for a year of the prophet Moses. It would be a year with numerous deaths: men and women, children and old folks—many would die that year. There would also be illness, strife, and war. Heavy rains would fall and hard winds would blow, and the storms would claim many lives.

That afternoon we talked with Sanogo about the dire nature of the predictions. Everything he had read aloud that morning, he assured us, meant one thing only: you should ask God for protection—in other words, you should recite gaara—and also give saraa. That was the main thing.

"*S*ome marabouts have a book or manuscript with new year's tidings, which they read to people, but this is not in accordance with our religion," Abdoulaye Touré informed me a few days after we had first heard Hamidou Sanogo reading from the jiiri-fita. We had broached the subject by telling him that I'd heard that there were places in town where predictions for the new year were read on ashura. He had heard the same, he said, but he claimed not to know where or by whom these readings were given. While he did have a book of new year's tidings, he was careful to emphasize that he never read aloud from them. Nor did anyone come to ask him for predictions, for it was known that he would not reveal them. It was against the rules of Islam, because—as he continually stressed in our talks about the various methods of divination—only God knows what the future holds in store. It wasn't good to talk about it. "You predict that something will happen, and then it doesn't," said Touré. "Only God knows!"

Baba Toumagnon (1916–2000)

Chapter 6

The Milkmaid
and the Amulet

 $\mathcal{S}$ he was pretty, about eighteen years old and, in Boubakar's opinion, just right for me. Fatimata showed up around 8:00 PM, as she had done every evening for the past few days. Balancing a milk-filled calabash on her head, she stood at the top of the stairs, at the entrance to the veranda. A moment before, her high voice had resounded through the street: "Fresh milk, I have fresh milk."

We beckoned her over, and her slender form detached itself from the shadows. She asked if I wanted some milk, lifted the calabash from her head with an elegant movement, set it on the ground, and removed the wicker lid. I handed her an enamel bowl. Squatting down, she measured the milk with a small calabash ladle. I studied her face. She had the fine features and slightly lighter skin of the Fulbe women. Her hair lay in tight braids against her head, and wisps of it stuck out from under her head-scarf. One of her tiny earrings glinted faintly in the reflected light of the oil lamp. She glanced at me with her almond-shaped eyes, but I swiftly lowered my gaze and focused on the milk.

After ladling eight measures of milk into my bowl, she stopped. It was the usual amount: enough to boil the next morning to make Nescafé for Boubakar and me. While I was fishing around in my wallet for two 100-franc coins, Boubakar repeated to Fatimata his teasing remarks of the last few evenings, saying that she should stay a bit longer so we could talk. Fatimata laughed shyly and said she had to go, since she still had to sell the rest of the milk. Picking up her calabash, she disappeared into the darkness of the stairwell with her usual grace.

85

As soon as Fatimata was gone and we could hear her voice again in the street, Boubakar returned to the subject that had been occupying him recently: as a man on my own, surely I was missing something. I'd been living in Djenné now for six months. Didn't I feel lonely sometimes? And hadn't I said, after Fatimata's first visit, that she was pretty? The conversation took its usual course, alternating between curiosity about my ideas on the subject and outright joking.

The following evening, a young marabout named Sidi Oumar joined us on the veranda. We had become friendly with him, and he regularly came over to chat. Sidi, who was in his early thirties, had left his native village and come to Djenné to study at one of the schools for advanced Qur'anic instruction. In his village he had attended not only a Qur'anic school but also a French school. Our meetings were more lively and relaxed than those at which Boubakar had to act as interpreter.

At around 8:00 PM our conversation was interrupted by the appearance of Fatimata on her daily milk run, but she was more than welcome. Trying to conceal the flurry of anticipation occasioned by her arrival, I set my milk bowl down next to her calabash and crouched across from her while she ladled the milk into the bowl. I didn't understand a word of what Sidi and Boubakar were saying, but their remarks made Fatimata giggle in embarrassment.

This time, following Fatimata's short visit, I had two well-meaning advisors to contend with. Sidi and Boubakar were in complete agreement: I was in need of a female companion. Finding the situation highly entertaining, they fired questions at me and offered advice. Sidi said that if I was willing, he could arrange for Fatimata to fall in love with me. He could make me a *gris-gris*, an amulet, which would make something happen between me and the milkmaid. I accepted Sidi's offer, and to my surprise, he did not refuse my request to watch him make the amulet, and even promised to do it at my house.

*S*everal days later Boubakar brought me a little bottle filled with a slightly cloudy liquid, which Sidi Oumar had asked him to give me. The bottle contained *nesi* (amulet water), that is, water in which an amulet text had been dissolved. Sidi had used this water to wash the text off his writing board. Boubakar told me to dab some on my head now and then, or drink it, if I preferred. The nesi fulfilled only part of Sidi's promise. Later that day he would come over to make the rest of the amulet.

Around 6:30 that evening—it was already growing dark—Sidi arrived. He asked if I had a mat for him, and if he could use the brazier and some charcoal. When the charcoal was burning, he carried the brazier over to the mat in the middle of the veranda, placed it on a low stool, and sat down next to it. From a small plastic bag he took several grains of incense and threw them onto the fire. Then he reached into the pocket of his robe, produced a piece of paper with some writing on it, and held it for several seconds above the brazier. The fragrant smoke curled around its edges.

Sidi then folded the paper into a small square, felt around in his pocket, pulled out a long cotton thread, and wound some of it around the tightly folded paper. To the end of the thread he fastened a pin, which he pushed into the mud ceiling directly above the brazier. And there the paper hung, about half a meter above the glowing embers, in the heat rising from the fire.

When he was through, Sidi turned toward Mecca and began the prostrations that accompany Islamic prayer. *Allahu akbar*, God is great, resounded softly across the veranda. After the prayer he recited a number of formulas, seated cross-legged in front of the brazier. Then he picked up his prayer beads (tasbiya).

While slowly letting the string glide through the fingers of his right hand, Sidi counted the beads between his thumb and forefinger, mumbling a few words at every bead. He continued to sit there, imperturbable, repeating the same line over and over again. The cadence of his monotonal murmurs marked the tempo at which the string of beads glided through his fingers. Each time he came to the end of the 99 beads, he shifted one of the smaller beads above the tassel. Every once in a while he threw a handful of incense onto the burning coals.

Darkness began to fall. From time to time the glowing coals lit up Sidi's face, but otherwise his features were indistinguishable in the dark. Later he told me how exhausting it had been to perform that long series of recitations.

More than an hour after Sidi had hung the folded paper from the ceiling, he took it down, wound the rest of the thread around it, and presented it to me. He explained that I could have a small leather pouch made for the amulet, and then I could either wear it or hang it in my house. After all, that was where Fatimata would presumably continue to visit me.

*I*n the weeks that followed the production of the love amulet, Sidi and I had a number of talks, during which he gradually revealed to me how he had made it. These sessions were special, all the more so in retrospect, after learning how uncommunicative marabouts usually are on this subject. On these occasions, Sidi would fill pieces of paper with magic squares and numbers, with sun positions and tables, with Arabic words and mysterious signs. I made every effort to understand it all, and to record it as faithfully as possible. At the same time, I had to make sure I did not seem too pushy or overly eager to acquire the secret knowledge he possessed. I had to stop asking questions whenever Sidi indicated—with a curt remark or a change in tone—that he either could not or would not say anything more on the subject, sometimes because he had reached the limits of his knowledge.

Sidi's account was fragmented and not always presented in a logical sequence. Only later was I able to piece together much of what we discussed.

"It is," Sidi remarked, "as the Prophet said, 'Take what you want from the Qur'an.'" The Yusuf sura, which recounts the story of Joseph, who was so handsome that the wife of his Egyptian master fell madly in love with him, contains the phrase: "he has infatuated her with ardent passion." Sidi pointed to this passage in my copy of the Qur'an and told me that these were the very words he had used in the love amulet. Indeed, this passage had played a key role throughout the production process, for it comprised the words Sidi had recited while seated in front of the brazier on my veranda. With the help of his prayer beads, he had carefully counted his repetitions of the phrase and had stopped after reciting the passage exactly 1,957 times—a number that was far from arbitrary.

As soon as a marabout decides which Qur'anic passage to use in an amulet, he calculates the numerical value of its words. Knowledge of numerology is therefore vital to the production of amulets. Sidi added up the numerical value of the individual letters to arrive at a total value of 1,957 for the line he had chosen from the Yusuf sura. This number was a determining factor in many of the stages involved in the making of the amulet. To begin with, it was used to designate the time at which the amulet text should be written.

"There is a specific time for every form of maraboutage," Sidi explained. "There is a time for good work and a time for bad work." Each of the seven days of the week can be divided into 24 planetary hours, 12 for the day and 12 for the night. Each of these periods falls under the sign of one of the seven planets or, more properly speaking, celestial bodies. The sun, the moon, and the planets Mars, Mercury, Jupiter, Venus, and Saturn each exert an influence on a certain part of the day or night. The hours under the sign of the sun, the moon, and the planets Jupiter and Venus are suitable for "good work." Under the signs of Mars and Saturn it is possible to carry out "bad work." And in an hour under the sign of Mercury, it is possible to do both "good work" and "bad work," the latter to be understood as things done to harm a person or thwart someone's plans.

Planetary hours differ in length from clock hours, since a planetary hour is exactly one-twelfth of the actual length of a day or night. At the time of year in which Sidi made the amulet, the day—from sunrise to sunset—lasted 12 hours and 45 minutes. The daytime planetary hours were therefore 64 minutes long (60 + the result of 45 divided by 12), whereas the nighttime planetary hours lasted 56 minutes.

To ensure that the correct astrological influences were at work while he was making the amulet, Sidi first calculated which planetary hour was appropriate for its production. To do this, he took the numerical value of the Qur'anic passage (1,957) and divided it by 12, which left a remainder of one. This told him that the first hour of the day was the ideal one, though at the time he was doing his calculations, this hour had already passed. Sidi then consulted a table of planetary hours to find the sign that belonged to the first hour considered most favorable that day, a Wednesday. It appeared to be an hour of Mercury. The next hours with the same characteristics were the fifth and twelfth hours of Thursday, so he postponed the writing of the amulet until the fifth hour of the following day, knowing that seven hours later he would have to begin the 1,957 recitations of the Qur'anic line "he has infatuated her with ardent passion."

The next day, when the favorable hour of Mercury had come, Sidi wrote the amulet text on a piece of paper. On one-half of a sheet from a notebook, he recorded various lines of text, seven signs, a nine-cell square, eight numerals, the Qur'anic passage, and several names. It was this paper that he later folded up and hung above the brazier (see figure 6.1).

At the top of the amulet paper were seven mysterious signs, of which the first—the one on the far right—was a pentagram. Sidi told me that he began all amulets with these signs, which were important in many forms of maraboutage. Together these seven signs form "the greatest name" (al-ism al-a'zam) of God (see figure 6.2 on p. 91). These signs can be traced all the way back to the prophet Solomon. They were his seals, and the five-pointed star adorned his ring. When earlier marabouts discussed the greatest name of God, Ali—Muhammad's son-in-law—had given them these signs and taught them how to pronounce the name. Ali knew everything there was to know about maraboutage. He is the source of all knowledge about these practices. The Arabic pronunciation of God's greatest name, as revealed by Ali, consists of a fairly literal description of the individual signs: "Three sticks in a row after the ring; and a mîm erased and mangled; then a ladder to climb to everything hoped-for, but it is not a ladder; and four fingers in a row; and a split hâ; and a turned wâw like the ear of a cup, though it is not a cup"—in which the mîm, the hâ, and the wâw are, respectively, the twenty-fourth, twenty-sixth, and twenty-seventh letters of the Arabic alphabet. Sidi explained that in certain kinds of maraboutage, when it was necessary to utter the al-ism al-a'zam, it was this formula that the marabout recited.

Immediately below the seven signs, Sidi wrote two lines of text. The first began with the familiar sura opening, "In the name of God, Merciful to all, Compassionate to each! It is You we worship, and upon You we call for help." The second line read, "O God, bless our master Muhammad and the family of our master Muhammad and grant them peace." The first line

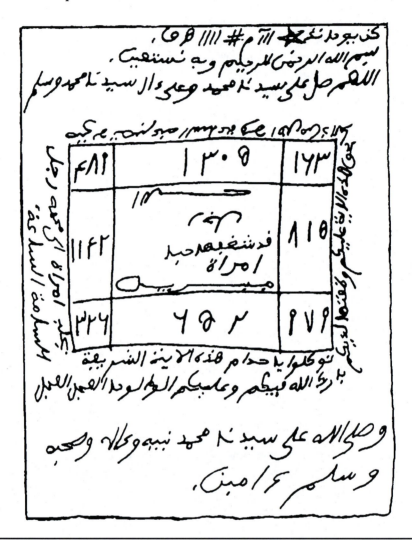

Figure 6.1   The text of the love amulet. In this example the names have been replaced by "man" (*rajul* in Arabic) and "woman" (*imra'a* in Arabic).

is a petitionary prayer to God; the second line, the so-called *tasliya*, entreats God to bless the Prophet and his family. At the very bottom of the paper, Sidi wrote another tasliya. In conclusion, God was again entreated to bless the Prophet, his family, and his companions, and to grant them peace.

In the middle of the page was a so-called magic square: a numerical square divided into cells, whose rows—horizontal, vertical, and diagonal—all yield the same sum. To explain the principle of such a square, Sidi drew its simplest form, in which all the rows add up to 15 (see figure 6.3).

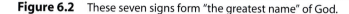

Figure 6.2   These seven signs form "the greatest name" of God.

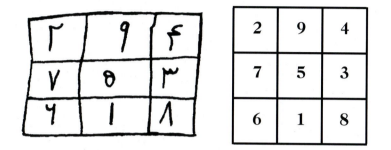

Figure 6.3   Example of a magic square, where each column and row yields the same sum.

Eight of the nine cells in the amulet's magic square contained numerals. The cell that occupied the central position in the amulet contained the Qur'anic passage "he has infatuated her with ardent passion" and four names. Above the line from the Qur'an was written—upside down—the name of the man for whom the amulet was intended, along with the name of God. Below it was written the name of the woman whose heart was to be conquered, along with the name of the angel Jibril. The names "Fatimata" and "Gérard" were thus oriented top to top, Sidi explained, so that they would attract each other and ultimately, too, the people they represented. If the names were written the other way around, with the man's name right side up and the woman's name upside down, they would be oriented bottom to bottom and thus repulse each other, which would be of no use in a love amulet.

The other eight cells contained numerals derived from the numerical value (1,957) of the Qur'anic passage written in the central cell. The calculations that make up each cell are based on the order in which they are filled.

As an example, Sidi drew a square on a piece of scrap paper, then filled it in (figure 6.4). He explained his calculations as follows:

- cell 1 = the numerical value divided by 12
- cell 2 = twice the number in cell 1
- cell 3 = three times the number in cell 1

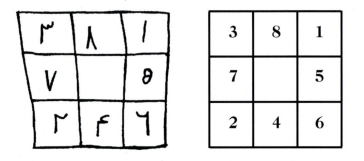

Figure 6.4   The calculations that make up each cell are based on the order in which they are filled.

- cell 4 = the sum of the numbers in cells 1 and 3
- cell 5 = the sum of the numbers in cells 1 and 4
- cell 6 = the sum of the numbers in cells 1 and 5, plus the remainder of the numerical value divided by 12
- cell 7 = the sum of the numbers in cells 1 and 6
- cell 8 = the sum of the numbers in cells 1 and 7

By using this method, each horizontal and vertical row of the square adds up to 1,957: the numerical value of the chosen passage from the Qur'an (see figure 6.5).

Devising this numerical square, Sidi explained, was the equivalent of writing "he has infatuated her with ardent passion" 1,957 times. Not only did it mean less work, but constructing a magic square had another advantage as well: numerical squares can easily be read by spirits, who understand their meaning at a glance.

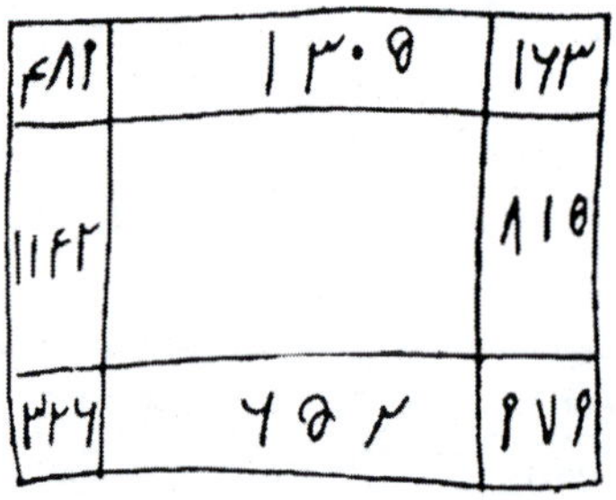

489	1305	163
1142		815
326	652	979

Figure 6.5   Each row of the square adds up to 1,957: the numerical value of the chosen Qur'anic passage.

Outside the numerical square, Sidi wrote a few lines addressed to the spirits: "Guarantee, servants of this noble verse, Fatimata's attraction to Gérard, so that she does not have to forgo his love, not even for an hour, owing to the strength of this verse and the protection it gives. God bless you. You must make haste, quickly, quickly now." Sidi also pronounced this text a number of times several hours later. After reciting "he has infatuated her with ardent passion" for the seventh, fiftieth, one hundredth, and every successive one hundredth time, he had urged "the servants of this noble verse" to act quickly to ensure that these two people would be attracted to each other.

"There are two kinds of spirits," Sidi explained, "lower spirits and higher spirits." The former are the djinns, whom God created from fire, as it says in the Qur'an. They can be found everywhere on earth and in the sea. No one knows how many of them there are, but one thing is certain: they outnumber the human beings in the world. They resemble humans in that they are capable of doing both good and evil. The higher spirits, by contrast, never do evil. Their behavior is exemplary. These are the angels (*malaika*), who are closest to God. They live scattered throughout the seven heavens. To seven angels and seven djinns God gave the responsibility to oversee everything on earth. A pair (one angel and one djinn) rules for one day a week, and together all seven constitute "the reign of God." Other spirits cannot do anything, good or evil, without the permission of these "kings." It was therefore important that Sidi, before invoking the "servants" of the chosen Qur'anic passage, ask permission from the kings in power that day. He did this by means of a special formula, which he recited seven times.

"The servants of the noble verse" also had names. From the Qur'anic passage used in the amulet, Sidi deduced the names of the leaders of all the angels and djinns bound by that particular passage. The names of djinns always have the suffix -*taysu*, the numerical value of which is equal to 319 (*tâ'* = 9; *yâ'* = 10; *sîn* = 300). This number is subtracted from the numerical value of the Qur'anic passage used, and the result is again transposed into letters. In the case of the love amulet, this means the following: 1,957 − 319 = 1,638. This number corresponds to the following letters: *ghain* = 1,000, *khâ'* = 600, *lâm* = 30, and *hâ'* = 8. Thus, the leader of all the djinns bound by the line "he has infatuated her with ardent passion" answered to the name of *Ghakhalahataysu*. By following this method, but taking the suffix -*â'îl*, which characterizes the names of the angels, Sidi ascertained that the name of his companion angel was *Ghazawa'il*.

After reciting exactly 1,000 times the words "he has infatuated her with ardent passion," he invoked this djinn-angel pair. He asked the djinn Ghakhalahataysu three times "on behalf of" the angel Ghazawa'il to ensure that what was written in the amulet would come to pass. Sidi uttered the names of both spirits. He explained that invoking the angel as well made it impossible for the djinn to ignore his request. The hierarchical relationship between angels and djinns was such that the djinn had to obey whenever the name of his companion angel was uttered. For his part, Ghakhalahataysu—the leader of all the djinns bound by that particular Qur'anic passage—would put his assistants to work.

But djinns and angels cannot be summoned just like that. As Sidi put it, "You can't invite someone over without offering him a meal." This also explains why he burned the incense: it is food for the spirits. Before Sidi could appeal to the "servants" of the Qur'anic passage, he had to make an offering of incense. To determine what kind of incense would be suitable, he turned once more to the numerical value of the chosen Qur'anic text, and by various calculations and transpositions of numbers into letters, he tried to find the name of the appropriate incense. This did not produce immediate results—something that happened often. In such cases there was a table that listed, for each day of the week, one or more kinds of incense that could be used as a suitable offering on that particular day. In my case Sidi had resorted to the incense listed for Thursday, the day he made the amulet: *djâwi* (benzoin resin). He was reconciled to it by the fact that one of its letters corresponded to a letter that had emerged from his calculations.

After writing out the text of the love amulet, Sidi made two copies of it: one in ballpoint pen on paper, the other in pen and ink on a writing board. The paper copy was intended for the spirits. Since they were supposed to come and fetch it, it was important to know where to deposit this copy. There were four possibilities, each associated with one of the elements. The paper could be buried in the ground (earth); it could be hung high up in a tree (air); it could be buried at the bottom of a river, stream, or pond, or along their shores (water); or it could be buried in a place where there was a hearth, such as a kitchen (fire). Sidi reckoned that, of these four, the appropriate element for the love amulet was "water." This was the element in which the spirits he had invoked would order their assistants to search for the paper. As soon as his calculations—for which the numerical value of the chosen Qur'anic passage again served as a basis—yielded this result, Sidi placed the amulet paper in a plastic bag and buried it along the shore of a tributary of the Bani River, just outside Djenné. The second copy of the amulet text, written in pen and ink, had been washed off the writing board to make the little bottle of nesi that Boubakar had brought me.

*A*fter Sidi gave me the love amulet—folded up, with thread wrapped around it—Boubakar took it to a leatherworker, who sewed it into a small pouch. A few days later I drove a nail into the wall above the door to my study, which, I figured, was as good a place as any to hang the amulet.

The amulet was ready. Fatimata continued to stop by on her daily rounds in the evenings, and Boubakar and I continued to drink Nescafé with milk in the mornings. As far as I was concerned, things could have gone on like this for a long time, but then something happened: a couple of days in a row, the milk curdled. One evening I tried to make it clear to Fatimata that I didn't want to buy spoiled milk. It was a difficult conversation. Fatimata spoke very little French, and my Songhay did not stretch to a discussion of curdled milk. What's more, I had to tackle this problem on my own, since Boubakar had stopped coming around after dinner, reasoning that his presence would reduce the amulet's effectiveness. Still, the only thing blossoming between Fatimata and me at that moment was the growing realization that we were unable to communicate. Our sole topic of conversation thus far—and even then, we were forced to rely on gestures—had been milk: milk which for several days now had not been fresh.

One morning, as I sat at my desk, working on my notes while waiting for Boubakar, I was startled by the sudden appearance of Fatimata in the doorway of my study. I stopped writing, mesmerized by the sight of her standing there, with my amulet hanging above her head. All sorts of thoughts flashed through my mind, but there was no time to come up with a plan. The magic of the moment vanished instantly when Fatimata made the most prosaic remark imaginable: I owed her money. Again, communication was extremely difficult, the more so because my recollection of the amount I owed did not tally with hers.

After this, Fatimata's visits became less frequent. She showed up once or twice in the evening or early morning to ask if I wanted some milk, but apparently she no longer had much reason to visit me, just as I no longer showed much interest in her milk.

When Fatimata's visits had almost stopped, I broached the subject of the amulet with Sidi and Boubakar. Had it worked? As far as they were concerned, it had. Hadn't Fatimata come to my house? Yes. And what had I done? Had I done all I could to help things along? Had I seized every opportunity that presented itself? In such cases you had to leap into action, not wait for matters to take their course.

After that the subject was never mentioned again. Until the end of my first year in Djenné, months after Fatimata—with her milk-filled calabash and her almond-shaped eyes—had stopped coming to see me, the amulet continued to hang in my study, a silent witness to that unforgettable day when Sidi Oumar, seated on the veranda, had recited "he has infatuated her with ardent passion" 1,957 times.

Ibrahim Traoré, also known as Bio Bio (1922–2006)

Chapter 7

Amulets

*T*oward the end of the eighteenth century, the Scottish explorer Mungo Park led an expedition through the unknown interior of West Africa. He had been sent by the African Association of London to chart the course of the Niger River. In his account of the journey, Park (1983[1799]) described his arrival at dusk on the evening of August 20, 1797, in the market town of Koulikoro—approximately 50 kilometers northeast of Bamako—where he found accommodation in the house of a trader. He had scarcely settled in when his host, a Muslim, approached him with the following request:

> When he heard that I was a Christian, he immediately thought of procuring a *saphie* [i.e., amulet], and for this purpose brought out his *walha*, or writing board, assuring me, that he would dress me a supper of rice, if I would write him a saphie to protect him from wicked men. The proposal was of too great consequence to me to be refused; I therefore wrote the board full from top to bottom on both sides; and my landlord, to be certain of having the whole force of the charm, washed the writing from the board into a calabash with a little water, and having said a few prayers over it, drank this powerful draught; after which, lest a single word should escape, he licked the board until it was quite dry.

A short while later the son of the village chief also came to see Park, because, as the explorer sensed, "a saphie writer was a man of too great consequence to be long concealed." The village chief wanted an amulet to help him amass a fortune, and had sent along half a sheet of paper for this purpose. In exchange for the text, the chief sent Park some milk and flour.

Mungo Park's eighteenth-century experiences underscore the main characteristic of the amulets still produced by marabouts today. Unlike

97

the traditional African charms that contain pieces of bone, skin, tree bark, roots, or other animal or vegetable material as the bearer of special powers, Islamic amulets derive their power from a written text. The importance of the writing is illustrated by the reason I was sometimes given for an amulet's ineffectiveness: it would not work if even "a single pen stroke" of its text was incorrect; it was vital, when writing down the words, to make sure that nothing was forgotten.

According to the French Islamologist Edmond Doutté, who published a standard reference work on Islam in North Africa in 1909, it is easy to understand why the written word is thought to have special powers. After all, a transcription of spoken words is much easier to manipulate and much more permanent than speech itself. Transforming intangible speech into tangible letters makes it possible to take full advantage of the magical powers ascribed to spoken formulas. Not only can a written text be carried around or stashed away somewhere, but the writing itself can be subjected to various treatments. Words can be written in a variety of ways: horizontal or vertical, right side up or upside down, from front to back or back to front. A sentence can be split up and its component parts arranged in a geometric shape. All these permutations heighten the mysterious nature of the writing. It is therefore only natural, in Doutté's opinion, to attribute it with magical powers.

Although it is mainly the characteristics of written words that make them suitable for inclusion in an amulet, the language used in an Islamic amulet is also important, for it too has special properties. The Arabic used in amulets is the language of the Qur'an, which is believed to be the literal word of God.

Several days after the celebration of Muhammad's name day (almudu), Boubakar and I had a talk with Abdoulaye Touré. We spoke about the Arabic poems of praise that the marabout and others had recited every evening for more than two weeks. This prompted Touré to dwell on the special nature of the Arabic language. Arabic, he told us, is the oldest language in the world, with the oldest script. Both spoken and written Arabic were revealed by God's angels to Adam, the first man. Every other script is man-made and of later origin. Arabic is the language in which the Holy Qur'an was sent down to Muhammad, and is thus the language of the Prophet in whose honor the world was created. Arabic is spoken in "the other world," and on "the well-preserved tablet" that is kept in heaven, on which everything that has happened, is now happening, and ever will happen, as ordained by God, is written in Arabic.

In a sermon (waaju) he gave on Muhammad's name day, Alfa Baba Kampo stressed the mythical origins of Arabic, whose script formed the basis of man's creation, since the human figure was patterned on Arabic characters. Even before the world was created, Muhammad's name, written in Arabic, was with God, and He created man in the image formed by these letters. The Arabic word— محمد —"Muhammad" consists of four letters: a mîm, a hâ, another mîm and a dâl. The first mîm served as the model for the human head, the hâ for the arms, the second mîm for the torso, and the dâl for the legs. For this reason too, Kampo told his audience, those who are doomed will never enter hell in their human shape. Sinners go to hell in the shape of a ball, with no head, arms, or legs, for the name of the Prophet shall never burn in hell.

𝓜arabouts write amulets for many purposes. People seeking protection from evil or disease, those hoping to acquire riches or power, childless women hoping to conceive, men in search of a wife—they can all go to a marabout and ask him to write an amulet. Amulets that are worn on the body (in a wrapping of leather or cloth) or hung in the house are called *tira*. The powers attributed to them are also present in liquid form. Nesi, the water with which an amulet text has been washed off a writing board, can be drunk, dabbed on parts of the body, or added to bathwater. Amulets can even be inhaled in the form of smoke.

Abdoulaye Touré once told us about a Frenchman who had come to see him in the early 1980s. This Frenchman was visiting Sevaré, near

Two boys wearing amulets around their necks (photo taken by the author).

A man wearing a leather band containing an amulet around his upper arm (photo taken by the author).

Mopti, where he met a trader from Djenné. The two men got to talking, and the Frenchman said that for years he had been suffering from headaches so severe that they kept him awake at night. In France he had consulted various doctors, but no one had been able to relieve his pain. The trader told him about a marabout in Djenné who could cure him. Together they went to see Touré, with the trader acting as interpreter. Touré listened to the man's story and told him that he had a remedy that he would give him, along with instructions for its use. If it proved effective, the man would have to pay him 50,000 francs. The Frenchman said that money was no issue, and—eager to be rid of his headaches—paid the entire amount immediately. Touré gave him a few pieces of dried tree bark, "prepared in a special way." At the Hotel-Campement, where the Frenchman was staying, he asked for a brazier with glowing coals. Touré had instructed him to put a cloth over his head, lean over the brazier, throw a couple of pieces of the tree bark on the fire, and breathe in the smoke—and to repeat this treatment in the evening before going to bed.

The next morning the Frenchman went to see Touré again. He had done exactly as he was told, and had slept better than he had for a long time, without the slightest trace of a headache. The man thanked Touré warmly, and the marabout gave him a bit more of the specially prepared bark, to use back in France if the need should arise. Later on Touré received three letters from the man, who appeared to be completely cured.

Years before this Touré had given the same medicine to a man from Bamako, who was having such trouble waking up in the morning that he slept through several alarm clocks. That time, too, the medicine had the desired effect. He had charged the man from Bamako 2,500 francs for his services.

The same medicine could be prescribed in both cases, Touré explained, because both complaints—headaches and an inability to wake up—were in the head. When the medicine was inhaled, its healing vapors entered the head directly.

We asked Touré about his "special way" of preparing this particular medicine. The marabout replied that he had sprinkled the tree bark with nesi. "There are four places in the Qur'an where God utters words that can act as a remedy for complaints like the one the Frenchman was suffering from," he added.

A Qur'anic text suitable for use in an amulet can be anything from a short sura to a single word. A special category of such words are the so-called 99 "beautiful names" (al-asmâ al-husnâ) of God. Epithets such as the First, the Last, the Manifest, and the Hidden, and names that include the Creator, the King, the Judge, the Friend, the Merciful One, and the Compassionate One, all figure among the 99 names of God compiled by Islamic scholars. The Qur'an contains the passage, "The most beautiful names belong to Allah: so call on him by them" (7:180). The names of God are thought to have special powers.

In one of our talks about the production of the love amulet, Sidi Oumar told us that such amulets could contain the name *al-Wadud* (the Loving One). But there were other names of God that were also suitable for use in amulets: *al-Hafiz* (the Protector, the Guardian) could be used in an amulet intended to protect its wearer against illness, for example, and *al-`Alîm* (the Omniscient) was suited to boosting a pupil's intelligence. To illustrate the use of the name *al-`Alî* (the Exalted), Sidi told the following story.

Once, in Medina, an infidel came to Ali. Since Ali was famous for his strength in battle, the man assumed that he must know a great deal about maraboutage. He asked Ali to come up with something that would make him invincible, and showed him bags of gold and silver, which he had brought along as payment. Ali, who assumed that "the requests of infidels do not count," accepted the money, took a piece of parchment,

A group of boys a couple of days after being circumcised. In some cases the protective amulets they wear during this vulnerable period are clearly visible (photo taken by the author).

and wrote: "An infidel who had eaten his fill sought out Ali, brought him a fortune, and asked Ali to perform maraboutage, so that no one could defeat him." Ali folded the parchment into a small package and gave it to the man, who sealed it in wax and tied it to his head, under his hair.

Some time later the Prophet and his followers invaded the infidel's land. Ali and the man, whom he did not recognize, met in single combat. The two were well matched. Each time they fought—first with the sword, then the lance, and finally hand-to-hand—the struggle was undecided. Ali was perplexed, because he had never before encountered such resistance. Finally, he uttered a secret formula that contained the name of God, but when that, too, proved useless, he turned in desperation to the Prophet. Muhammad told Ali who his adversary was. Hadn't he himself once given this man something to make him invincible? Ali suddenly remembered the man, but he was still baffled, because he had given him a seemingly innocuous text. When he repeated the words he had written on the parchment, however, Muhammad pointed out that the name "Ali" occurred in the text. That name was far from innocuous, since al-`Alî (the Exalted) was one of the names of God. The Prophet explained that the man owed his invincibility to this name, and told Ali where the infidel wore his amulet. As soon as Ali pulled the amulet off the man's head, he won the battle.

*F*or centuries the great Islamic scholars have debated the question of whether Islam actually allows the practice of magic. Muhammad often warned his followers of the unreliability of diviners and sorcerers. Both the Qur'an and the hadîth advise Muslims to refrain from the practice of magic. Even so, Islam does not totally deny the efficacy of protective amulets and therapeutic magic. There are, in fact, traditions regarding forms of spiritual protection against evil (*ruqya*), of which the Prophet supposedly approved. Muhammad permitted the use of some chapters of the Qur'an to undo, by way of counter-magic, the effects of the evil eye and to heal the sick. This protective power is intrinsic to the revelation itself. In sura 17:82 it is written: "We send down from the Qur'an what is a remedy and a mercy to the faithful." Although this verse refers to spiritual healing, it is also thought to betoken the Qur'an's power to cure physical complaints.

Even if one does not doubt the protective power of the Qur'an, the legality of making amulets based on this power has always been a subject of debate. When the fifteenth-century Algerian-born jurist al-Maghili went to Gao to visit the Songhay emperor Askia Mohammed, he even went so far as to issue orders forbidding all Muslims from making amulets, on pain of death. In his view the production of amulets was not only deceitful but also contradicted the teachings of the Qur'an and the traditions of the Prophet.

Still, there were others who were less strongly opposed to amulet-making. An example is Muhammad Bello, the nineteenth-century leader of the Sokoto Caliphate in northern Nigeria, who defended the Qur'an as an acceptable source of amulet texts. He maintained that a Qur'anic passage used in an amulet should be seen as an appeal to God to aid the owner of the amulet. Such amulets formed a du^câ', a petitionary prayer, by means of which the bearer of the amulet asked God for help.

*A*t our request Alfa Baba Kampo had compiled a list of the books read by the pupils at his majlisu. We discussed this list, which contained 36 books on such subjects as Islamic jurisprudence, Arabic grammar and literature, theology, the traditions of the Prophet, and Qur'anic exegesis. It seemed a suitable moment to broach a branch of knowledge never before mentioned in our talks, so I asked Boubakar to inquire whether the marabout also taught sirri. At the mere mention of the word, Kampo's manner changed, and our conversation came to a momentary halt. I shifted my position and kept my eyes fixed on the notebook lying before me on the mat. Kampo replied that he did not teach sirri.

"Is it forbidden?" we asked.

"Who told you that?" Kampo asked guardedly.

We told him about a little book I'd once leafed through at the bookseller's in the market square. It was a slender French volume about Islamic prayer, one of many books on the subject with titles like *La prière en islam* and *Comment faire la prière?* At the back of this book was something resembling a letter of recommendation, written by an imam from Senegal, if I remember correctly. He had expressed his disapproval of amulets, which, he claimed, were not compatible with the precepts of Islam.

"Who wrote it?" asked Kampo, immediately adding, "a Wahhabi, no doubt?"

I couldn't answer that question, so I decided to change tack. "What about 'the stars,' then?" we asked him. We had touched upon this subject the week before, and now I hoped to steer our conversation, by way of astrology, back to the topic of sirri. The marabout replied that, as far as the stars were concerned, there were two "paths": astronomy and astrology. He elaborated on them briefly.

"And what's the general opinion about 'working' with buruj, the signs of the zodiac?" we asked.

The marabout's reply was curt and rather cryptic, "Some get results, others don't." It was a topic he clearly wished to avoid. Sirri is secret knowledge, and secrets are not disclosed, at least not without good reason. Kampo's response to the question of whether sirri was forbidden was therefore revealing. By sidestepping the issue—distracting our attention to the Wahhabis—he made it clear, without giving away his own thoughts on the matter, that there were those, such as the reformists in the Wahhabi movement, who unequivocally condemned the practice of amulet-making.

*M*arabout Moussa Tanapo was known for his sermons (waaju), which he delivered all over Mali and even in Abidjan. Every year, Tanapo spent a couple of weeks explaining the precepts of Islam at gatherings of his fellow townspeople. This year, in Djenné's market square on a series of Thursday evenings, he illustrated his sermons with stories from the lives of the prophets and verses from the Qur'an. One evening, while

Tanapo was enthralling his audience with a speech on the name of God, which is written in the heavens and in paradise, he suddenly permitted himself—as he often did—a short digression. "Shouldn't a person be allowed to invoke the name of God?" he exclaimed. "They say it's idolatry! Shouldn't a person be allowed to wear an amulet? They say it's a fetish! Is that true? In the name of God, I'm telling you that His name is not a fetish! We wear the names of God. We do this to seek protection. What about you? Don't you seek protection by carrying someone's name with you? Let's suppose you've forgotten your identity card. Whose name is on it? Surely it has a name! Isn't it true that we carry this card to protect ourselves from the police when we're traveling? Isn't that so? Just try and travel without an identity card and see how the police treat you. We always carry a name with us, so carry the name of God too. Carry it! Carry it!"

I had recorded Tanapo's speech, and later, when Boubakar and I were translating it, I asked him who Tanapo had meant by "they." We'd talked about them before, Boubakar said. Everyone knew that in this case "they" were the Wahhabis, who forbade the wearing of amulets.

"But God sent us amulet texts for a reason," he said, and proceeded to tell me how the Prophet had once rid himself of his enemies with the help of a passage from the Qur'an. One night, after Muhammad and his companions had lain down to rest, they were surrounded by enemies. God therefore gave a text to the angel Jibril with instructions to take it to the Prophet. The Prophet took a handful of sand, repeated the text the angel had conveyed to him, spit gently on the sand, and threw it at his besiegers, who immediately fell to the ground. The text that had saved Muhammad could be found in the Qur'an, in the *Ya Sin* sura, though Boubakar did not know the exact lines. He had heard this story from a marabout. It was an example of the efficacy of words from the Qur'an. Indeed, similar examples could be found in the lives of other prophets—Joseph, thrown in a well; Abraham, laid on a pyre by unbelievers; Jonas, stuck in the stomach of the whale—to all of whom God revealed a text that enabled them to escape from a perilous situation.

"It is just as God said in His great Book," Boubakar added. "In the Qur'an, the things that have come down to us from heaven are like medicine and happiness to those who believe." And after leafing through my Qur'an, he pointed out the exact passage: "We send down from the Qur'an what is a remedy and a mercy to the faithful" (17:82).

One afternoon I decided to approach this subject in a more structured way. We had often talked about amulets, which we usually referred to as gris-gris, the term used throughout French West Africa. The subject of amulets had cropped up repeatedly in my conversations with Boubakar, as well as in our talks with marabouts such as Sidi Oumar. They had mentioned several forms, varying in both type and use. Seated at the table in my study, with my notebook before me, I asked Boubakar for an explanation.

"There are three kinds of amulets," Boubakar began. "Some are known as *alhidjaba*, others as *Yer Koy naarey*, and still others as *dabari*."

He watched as I wrote down the three terms, and then continued. "Alhidjaba offer protection from the dangers that threaten people or their homes. They are worn on the body, hung in the house, or buried under the threshold. They offer protection from sickness and misfortune, from evil spirits and bad people, from thieves and fire."

"Are marabouts the ones who make alhidjaba?" I asked.

"Absolutely."

"Could anyone make something similar?"

"Of course, if they have the text. But ultimately it comes from a marabout, because he's the one who gives you the text."

The second category, Boubakar explained, actually encompasses all amulets. Yer Koy naarey literally means "asking or entreating God." Boubakar continued. "The important parts—words taken from the Qur'an, the names of God—all of that is Yer Koy naarey, because when we invoke God's name, we're asking Him to listen to us. In fact, everything is Yer Koy naarey, but the work called by that name can serve many purposes, such as insuring that someone is well-loved, raising a pupil's intelligence, allowing a certain team to win a boat race, making the rains come, guaranteeing a good harvest—so that everyone in the family has enough to eat—or curing someone of a specific disease."

"Is Yer Koy naarey the work of marabouts?"

"In theory, yes, Yer Koy naarey is the work of marabouts. Of course if you know how to do it, you can do it yourself, but like they say, 'You can't shave your own head cleanly.' You can't always solve your own problems; sometimes you need to ask others for help. As another saying goes, 'No matter how sharp a knife, it can't carve its own handle.'"

Boubakar was very brief on the subject of dabari, the third kind of amulet. "When you hear the word dabari, the first thing you think of is something bad," he said. "Dabari can be used maliciously to harm people, to make them fall ill, or even to kill them. There are nesi that can protect you from assailants. If someone dabs or washes his head with it, and is then struck by another person, that person will die within a week."

Sidi Oumar had also spoken of "bad work" when he told me about a former imam of Djenné. At the time it was said that he was a bad person, and most people were afraid of him. But it was not that simple, Sidi said,

because he knew for a fact that the imam had only been reacting to prov-
ocation. Once a marabout, who was determined to harm the imam in
some way, drew a magic square on the palm of his right hand. If only he
could manage to bring it into contact with the imam while shaking his
hand, "something bad" would befall the imam. The opportunity finally
presented itself: an occasion where much handshaking was going on. The
marabout stood aloof, anxiously keeping his hand beneath his robe until
he met the imam. The two men shook hands, whereupon the marabout
screamed and jerked his hand away from the imam's. He cried out with
pain as his right arm began to swell from hand to elbow. The imam had
known exactly what the marabout was planning to do, and had been prepared for it. In fact, he never left the house unprepared. He consulted the
turaabu, for example, and took measures to ward off any evil he sus-
pected he might encounter.

Sidi told me that the use of dabari was sometimes necessary. For
instance, if a person had been warned at least three times by a marabout
that he was acting against God's precepts, he would have good reason to
fear that the marabout would "do something" to harm him.

Dabari literally means "to prepare" or "to take measures." Later on
in this same talk with Boubakar, I returned to the intriguing example of
an amulet made to help a team win a boat race. Boubakar told me that
the various teams participating in the annual *pirogue* races on the Bani
River—due to take place several weeks later, during the independence
day celebrations on September 22—would prepare themselves in all kinds
of ways. One way was to ask a marabout to make them an amulet. What
kind of amulet it was depended on one's point of view. The team that
ordered the amulet could consider it Yer Koy naarey, since winning was a
good thing. But from their opponents' perspective, that amulet would be
dabari, because it worked to their disadvantage. Even in the case of an
amulet made to help a man find a wife, Boubakar explained, that amulet
could be seen as both Yer Koy naarey and dabari. Here as well, there
were two sides to the story. But, he added, "raising a pupil's intelligence"
or "asking for rain" could never be considered dabari, since such things
could do no harm.

Another practice that falls in the category of dabari, or the "bad
work" marabouts sometimes do, is "to fabricate money." Accumulating
money or gold with the help of sirri knowledge is morally reprehensible;
it runs counter to the idea that a person must work for a living. Boubakar
asked me if I remembered the story he had recently told me about Alfa
Kosoukoré. I had asked him to name a number of great marabouts, and
one of the first that had occurred to him was Alfa Kosoukoré from the village of Tiye, some forty-five kilometers northeast of Djenné. Boubakar

had told me the following story about this well-known marabout, who died in the early 1980s.

One day a marabout came to Tiye, looking for Alfa Kosoukoré, whose fame had spread far beyond his village. When the man found Kosoukoré's house, he was told that the famous marabout was out working in the field. He asked the way, and when he reached the field, he found Kosoukoré hoeing. After Kosoukoré had eaten his midday meal, he rested for a while, waiting for the hour of prayer. It was then that the man approached him.

"O marabout, why is a great marabout like you still tilling the fields? I'll give you a text so that you can give up farming and take a well-deserved rest. You're too old for such hard work."

"That would please me greatly, go right ahead," Kosoukoré said to his visitor.

The man drew four squares in the sand, covered them with a rug, picked up his prayer beads, and started to recite his secret text. Slowly a bulge appeared in the rug, and as he recited, it ballooned even more. When the marabout had finished counting his prayer beads, he stopped reciting and pulled back the rug to reveal a huge stack of paper money, all of which, the man said, was for Kosoukoré.

Kosoukoré thanked his fellow marabout and asked if he might borrow his prayer beads. He drew a circle in the sand, covered it with the rug, and started counting the beads. The moment the first bead slid through his fingers, the rug began to bulge. At the second bead, it bulged a bit more, and at the third, even more. At that point he stopped, and lifted the rug to reveal a small date tree. It was about half a meter tall and covered with dates—too many to count—and each one was made of pure gold. "You see!" Kosoukoré said to the man. "I, too, have a secret text!" Kosoukoré had no need of the money the man had tried to give him, since he was every bit as capable of conjuring it up himself. "But," he said, "I want to work for my wage. That's the best way, just as God commanded."

"One must suffer to live," Boubakar commented, repeating a line he often used.

Several weeks after this, Boubakar's older brother Mahaman also told me a story about Alfa Kosoukoré of Tiye, likewise involving a man who wanted to teach the famous marabout how to do something. And again Kosoukoré had taught his visitor a lesson by showing him that using maraboutage to garner riches was despicable. In contrast to the first story, however, in Mahaman's tale the riches—in this case a gold chain—had been stolen. The incident thus involved an injured party, as in all cases of dabari.

Mahaman's story went as follows. Once a marabout approached Kosoukoré and asked if he could show him something. When Kosoukoré agreed, the visitor "recited a text in the palm of his hand," meaning that he mumbled a text while holding his hand in front of his mouth, after which he spit gently into his hand and waved it in the air. Suddenly a gold chain appeared in his hand. The marabout handed the chain to Kosoukoré and said it was a present. Kosoukoré refused to accept it.

When the visitor was about to leave, Kosoukoré said, "Wait, I have something to show you too!" He recited a text in the palm of his hand, then rubbed his hand over the face of the other marabout. At once the man saw a sobbing child standing some distance away. The little girl came over to them, and the marabout asked her what was wrong. The child replied that someone had just stolen her gold chain. The marabout gave it back to her, and she thanked him and left.

The girl, Mahaman explained, was a djinn that Kosoukoré had made visible to his visitor. Her chain had been taken from her by another djinn. Forms of maraboutage such as this always involved theft.

*Y*ousouf Traoré had spent a large part of the afternoon down in the courtyard with two fellow pupils, reading aloud from an Arabic book. When they left, Yousouf came upstairs to join us. Earlier that week he had mentioned that he wanted to talk to me about something. Boubakar brought a stool from the veranda and set it beside the table. Yousouf pointed to my notebook, which lay open on the table, and asked if I'd written enough for that day, because now he wanted to show me something.

He began by saying how long we'd known each other and how well we got along, and because I brought him a gift every time I returned to Djenné, he now wanted to give me something in return: "a text" I could use to fulfill my every wish.

Yousouf went on to say that he had decided to give me a text and instructions for its use, rather than simply making me an amulet, because an amulet would help me solve only one problem—the specific one for which it was made—whereas a text could be put to use whenever and wherever I needed it.

While Boubakar was translating Yousouf's words, the latter explained that I should begin by writing one of the last suras of the Qur'an 100 times. The first verse—"In the name of God, Merciful to all, Compassionate to each!"—only had to be written once. That line, followed by the tasliya used to invoke God's blessing for the Prophet—"O God, bless our master Muhammad and the family of our master Muhammad and grant them peace"—was to appear at the top of the page. Below these lines I was to write the rest of the sura 100 times, and then, by way of closing, end with a repetition of the prayer for the Prophet and his family.

Yousouf felt around in the pocket of his robe, pulled out a folded piece of paper, opened it up, and laid it on the table. On this paper he had drawn a square divided into 16 cells, each of which contained a number. In the middle, between the cells, was a small diamond-shaped space that had been left empty. Yousouf told me to copy this numerical square into the amulet text, below the lines from the Qur'an. In the middle, in the empty diamond, I was to write my "wish." Later, when I looked at the numbers in the square more closely, it proved to be a magic square in which the numbers 642 to 657 were placed in such a way that the horizontal, vertical, and diagonal rows always added up to 2,598.

Yousouf knew from previous conversations that I was looking for a house in the Netherlands. He therefore suggested that I write the word "house" in the middle of the square and advised me to add, if possible, the name of the present owner of the house I hoped to acquire or the name of someone who worked for the municipal authorities. The amulet was then supposed to be buried in the ground, either beneath or near the house I wanted, or else somewhere in the city or country where I was looking for a house. Yousouf stressed the importance of saying to myself, before writing my wish in the square, "May God grant me a house."

I wondered whether I was supposed to write my wish in Arabic. Boubakar asked Yousouf, who gave the question some thought. No, that wasn't necessary. If by chance I *could* write it in Arabic, then I should do so, by all means, but it wasn't essential. The important thing was to say to myself, "May God grant me a house."

"And it doesn't matter which language I say it in?" I asked.

"No, any language will do, that's not a problem," Yousouf replied. "It's the same with gaara," he went on to explain. "Those who speak Arabic recite gaara in Arabic, but those who don't speak Arabic can recite gaara in any language they please. It's wrong to say that Arabic gaara are better than gaara recited in other languages."

Yousouf asked if his instructions for making the amulet were clear. He promised to make a copy of the numerical square for me and give it to Boubakar.

A couple of days later I was sitting with Boubakar, poring over my copy of the magic square. We had gone over what Yousouf had said about making the amulet. Perhaps it would be of use to you as well, I said to Boubakar. His answer was brief: Yousouf had given the amulet to me, not to him.

When I was copying the square and its 16 numbers in my notebook, making sure to write the rows in the same order—namely from upper left to lower right—I asked Boubakar if this was really the correct way to fill in the square. He thought it best to consult Yousouf about this.

Late that afternoon we paid a visit to Yousouf and placed the magic square in front of him. He showed us how he had filled in the cells, starting with the lowest number and ending with the highest. Did I have to fill in the cells in this order, I asked him. "If you can," he said, "but it's not absolutely necessary."

Now that we were talking about the square, it occurred to me that Yousouf might be able to tell me how he had determined which numbers to use. Remembering what Sidi Oumar had told me about my love amulet, I wondered if there was a connection in this amulet between the sum of the magic square and the elements in its text. That sum must have been derived from something, I thought. In this case, however, there was no relationship between the "wish" the amulet was supposed to fulfill and the sum of the square, since this was a multipurpose square that could be put to many uses. I could also rule out the possibility that the number was the sum of the numerical values of the letters in the short sura that I was supposed to write in the amulet 100 times, because it was far too low a number for that. I also wondered why the sura had to be written 100 times, since that number bore no relation to the sum of the square. Was it simply a nice round figure, because the amulet was supposed to serve a variety of purposes? I asked Yousouf rather cautiously about the significance of the numbers, and he replied that he had received the square, just as it was, from his teacher, and that he knew nothing more about it. It had been given to him in the same way that he was now giving it to me.

Back in my study, I again asked Boubakar if he was sure he didn't want to make a copy of the magic square for himself. "Only if you really want to give it to me," he replied. "After all, it was given to you, not to me." When I assured him that I wanted him to have it, Boubakar laughed and admitted that he had copied it long ago—in fact, when Yousouf had first entrusted it to him, he had immediately made a copy before giving it to me. Surprised, I asked if we needed to go over the rest of Yousouf's explanation, the part about the square, but Boubakar didn't think so, since he had been there when Yousouf had explained it to me. Even though he already had a copy of the square, Boubakar said, it was important to him to receive it from me personally, just as I had received it from Yousouf, and Yousouf from his teacher.

*T*he very nature of the marabouts' secret knowledge makes it difficult to find out how they acquire and pass on their knowledge. The few marabouts who permitted me to broach the subject indicated that the teachers who had taught them to read the Qur'an were also the ones who had given them their first knowledge of sirri.

After a marabout has spent years teaching a pupil to read the Qur'an, he may decide to reveal some of his secrets to him, in which case he will give the pupil a number of written texts—including Qur'anic passages, names of God, mysterious signs, and numerical squares—and explain how and for what purpose these texts can be used. These first secret texts—or "amulet formulas," as they could be called, since they usually contain brief instructions on how and when to use them—form the beginning of a growing collection. Pupils who devote themselves to the study of sirri can go to other marabouts or remain for a while with their Qur'an teacher to add to their arsenal of secret knowledge. And what is true of bayaanu knowledge is equally true of sirri: continuing education is vital. There is always more to learn.

Knowledge of sirri can also be obtained from Arabic books and manuscripts, many of which come from North Africa or the Near East and are based on ancient handbooks of magic. Practitioners of maraboutage make use of both handwritten and printed sources. The degree to which they master this secret knowledge—all the facets of amulet production, for example—can vary greatly. This is clearly shown by the numerical square, which is an important part of many amulets. In writing an amulet, a marabout can make use of a ready-made square with the numbers already filled in. In that case he only has to search his collection for a square suited to the amulet's purpose. A marabout can also construct his own square, determining the numbers to be filled in by following cabbalistic rules to make calculations based on the numerical value of the Qur'anic text used in the amulet.

The differences in the marabouts' mastery of sirri can depend on how they obtained their knowledge. This, in turn, depends on their level of literacy in Arabic, acquired by studying at the advanced level at the Qur'anic school. The depth of the secret knowledge possessed by marabouts whose only resources are amulet formulas they have received from their teachers or have copied from the collections of others differs from that of marabouts whose knowledge of sirri has also been acquired by studying—whether or not under a teacher's supervision—the Arabic handbooks in which amulet production is described in detail.

Sidi Oumar told me that he had acquired his knowledge of amulet-making from three sources: the teacher in his native village who had taught him to read first the Qur'an and later books at an advanced level; a fisherman uncle who was also a marabout; and his own course of self-study. He told me that the most helpful book in this respect was *Ighâthat al-mazlûm wa-kashf asrâr al-'ulûm* (*The Rescue of the Wronged and the Revelation of the Secrets of Knowledge*), written by 'Abd al Fattâh al-Sayyid al-Tûkhî, general director of the astronomical institute Al-Futuh for Egypt and the East, published—as noted on the title page, which Sidi copied out for me—in Beirut, Lebanon. He explained that the "wronged" are the deceived pupils, who are forced by their incompetent teachers to pay good money for useless knowledge.

After a number of conversations in which we discussed the various stages of the love amulet's production, Sidi Oumar pointed out that no one book explains everything clearly. In fact, it is necessary to consult a number of books in order to acquire enough knowledge to carry out such work. Sidi had studied a variety of books together with his teacher. In many cases, he explained, a marabout gives his pupil only the numerical square for a certain kind of amulet, telling him that "the wish" should be written in the central cell, and perhaps also indicating how often and at what hours of the day a certain Qur'anic passage should be recited, but telling him nothing about the underlying calculations. In fact, this is not strictly necessary. The pupil keeps the square among his papers and copies it out whenever he needs it.

In Sidi's view, however, ready-made tables or squares are inferior. They are copied indiscriminately by those with no knowledge of the underlying system. Sometimes an amulet formula contains an intentional mistake, so that those who copy it will produce an ineffective and worthless amulet. Sidi stressed the fact that even the examples given in books sometimes contain deliberate mistakes; it is necessary to read the correct explanation very carefully and make sure you understand it.

The relative unimportance of Arabic literacy to amulet-making became clear when Boubakar's brother Mahaman—whose only education is several years of Qur'anic school—showed me a few examples from his personal collection of amulet formulas. Next to the texts and numerical squares he had written—in Songhay in Arabic script—catchwords such as "gold," "quarrel," and "wife" to indicate what the various texts were to be used for, so that he could choose the one he needed even though he couldn't read the Arabic explanation.

*S*everal days before Sidi Oumar and I began our talks about how he had made my love amulet, he told me the following story.

In the land of Shami (Syria), in the time between the prophets Jesus and Muhammad, there was a school where the pupils learned to make statues in wood and stone—statues that could speak. All the unbelievers sent their children to this school. There was a Jewish scholar who lived nearby, and one little boy passed his house daily on the way to school. The scholar's house was always brightly lit, though the boy never saw a lamp of any kind.

One day the boy entered the scholar's house and was given a warm welcome. He could see that the scholar lived well, that he prayed to God, and that he was pure. The boy was unaccustomed to praying to God; he was used to offering blood sacrifices to statues. He told the scholar that he wanted to learn how to pray and would like to become his pupil. The scholar agreed, and told him to start by learning the names of God.

While pretending to go to school, the boy went daily to the scholar's house. The scholar taught his pupil the names of God, one by one. When the boy had learned them all, his teacher said, "We are done." The boy was surprised, because he knew almost nothing of what the scholar knew. He asked his teacher which name, of all the ones he had learned, could be used to good effect: in other words, which was the greatest. But the scholar only answered, "All the names are good and great."

The pupil continued to nag his master, asking him repeatedly which of God's names was the greatest, but he never received a reply. One day he'd had enough, and angrily resolved to do his utmost to discover which name was the greatest. So he went home, locked the door behind him, and began to write all the names he had learned on tree leaves, using a separate leaf for each of God's names. When he was done, he lit a huge fire and tossed the leaves, one by one, into the fire, looking at each leaf first to see which name he'd written on it. Some of the leaves burned completely; others burned only on the unwritten side. One leaf, however, wouldn't burn at all. When he threw this leaf into the fire, it flew up out of the flames. Surprised, the boy threw the leaf into the fire again—and again the leaf escaped. He tried it a third time, but again the leaf flew up out of the flames. The pupil set this leaf aside for safe-keeping, and continued to toss leaves into the fire. Some of them burned completely; others burned only on the unwritten side. Finally, when all the leaves were gone, he threw the leaf he had set aside into the fire one last time. Again, it flew up out of the flames. Now he knew for sure that this was the greatest name of God! Everything the boy asked of God, invoking this name, would come true. That evening, he used this name to ask God for light, and his wish was granted.

The pupil went back to his teacher and said to him, "I've discovered the name you refused to give me." The scholar asked him how he had accomplished this. The boy told him about the leaves and the fire, and the scholar said, "You see, that's it. That's also how I discovered the greatest name of God. No one ever told me." That night the boy stayed with his teacher. When he awoke the next morning, the Jewish scholar had vanished without a trace.

Now, much later, as I reproduce this story, I see that I'm guilty of committing the methodological error I always warn my students about.

Nowhere in my field notes can I find a precise description of the in which Sidi Oumar told me this story. I failed to record anything the circumstances, the atmosphere, and, above all, the interaction between narrator and listener. In fact, all I can do is recount the story. Like the old Jewish scholar, the narrator's aim in telling the story has vanished into thin air. Was there a message in it for me? Did Sidi think it reflected the situation in which he found himself when confronted with a nosy anthropologist who was trying to pry secrets out of him? But let's not get lost in a forest of speculation.

Even so, there is one question we cannot avoid. Does the story of the Jewish scholar and his pupil tell us something about the working methods of marabouts? In their search for secret knowledge, do they make use of an experimental method comparable to the ordeal by fire undergone by the leaves? I doubt it. While the secret and idiosyncratic nature of such activities admittedly prevents us from making categorical statements, I think it unlikely that marabouts rely on such experimental methods. Instead, their knowledge of sirri is obtained from a teacher, by word of mouth, and by studying the relevant books.

What, then, is the crux of Sidi Oumar's story? Obviously various themes can be extracted from it, such as the teacher-pupil relationship, the importance of the written word, the fact that Jewish esoteric knowledge predates Islamic practices, the powers attributed to the names of God, and such oppositions as believer/unbeliever and purity/uncleanness. Above all, however, the story clearly shows that secret knowledge is not easy to obtain, that one must make an effort to acquire it. Determination and tenacity are required in any case. As Mamadou Waigalo once impressed upon me, perseverance and time—"a great deal of time"—are, according to Ali, two of the six prerequisites for "acquiring knowledge, true knowledge."

Boubacar (also known as Ko) Yaro (1942–1999)

Chapter 8

Beneficent Force and Almsgiving

"It's not right to sell God's name and make a living from it," a marabout replied when we asked if he performed maraboutage. It reminded me of what Sidi Oumar had told us about a former imam of Djenné. In his day this man had been renowned for his great knowledge of the secrets of maraboutage, and people were still telling stories about him: for example, how angry he became whenever anyone requested his help and immediately asked what it would cost. Unable to hide his annoyance, he would ask his client what on earth made him think he could place a monetary value on one word, or even one letter, of the Qur'an. His help cost what his clients could afford to give.

This prompted Sidi to express his disapproval of the changes that had taken place in the "business" of maraboutage. Things weren't what they used to be. Nowadays it was customary to discuss the price first, even before a marabout set to work for his client. The marabout generally began by asking an extremely high price. This was no way to treat the Word and the names of God, Sidi felt, and he was not alone in this. I heard many people voice similar complaints. Nevertheless, there is money to be made with maraboutage—in some cases a great deal of money.

One evening when Boubakar arrived late for supper, I was sitting in the courtyard of his parents' house, waiting for him. His mother had already set the meal in front of me: rice served in an enamel bowl with a wicker lid to keep it warm. After a while Boubakar appeared. While

117

bringing water so that we could wash our hands, he told me that he'd just been to see his sister and brother-in-law, and that they were having a large piece of grilled meat for supper. I lifted the cover off the bowl and looked at the three tiny fish nestled in a mound of rice and sauce. "They must be doing pretty well," I said.

Boubakar handed me the bowl of water. "What can you expect, after such a trip?" he replied.

His brother-in-law had just returned from a two-month stay in a village between Djenné and Mopti, where he had earned a tidy sum performing maraboutage for a number of clients.

As we dug into our rice, Boubakar began to talk about wealthy marabouts. There were marabouts in Bamako, he said, who lived in mansions, owned two Mercedes-Benzes, and walked around in grand boubous costing 100,000 francs. There were also marabouts who charged 1,000,000 francs for their services, and even then, a client would sometimes top it up with 500,000 more.

"That much?" My handful of rice stopped halfway to my mouth.

But Boubakar said I shouldn't be so surprised. It was only natural, after all. "If a marabout can help you earn 10,000,000 francs, surely you shouldn't mind paying him 1,500,000 francs?"

Now that the subject had turned to wealthy marabouts, the name of Abdoulaye Touré came up. Not long before this, during one of our weekly visits to him, Touré—who was telling us about the torrent of mail he received—suddenly stood up, went to an adjoining room, and returned with a plastic bag full of letters. It was the size of a large shopping bag. He put it in our hands for a moment, to let us feel how heavy it was. Touré said he sometimes received more than two hundred letters a year. Every Monday, the day the post arrived in Djenné, there were letters for him, sometimes four or five at a time. People from all over West Africa and Europe wrote to him, requesting his help, asking him to "work" for them, to perform maraboutage. Touré showed us the two letters he had received that week. One of them came from Ivory Coast, the other from France.

When Touré's far-flung clients requested treatment, he did the following: instead of preparing nesi in the usual way—by collecting the water used to wash an amulet text off a writing board—he wiped the text off with a damp wad of cotton, and mailed the inky-black wad to his client. All the client had to do to obtain the nesi was to dip the wad of cotton in some water and squeeze out the ink. In some cases, Touré also enclosed some "vegetable matter," which was bulkier. He then had to be very sure that his client would actually pay, because it cost 5,000 francs to send a parcel. Still, anyone who earned 200,000 francs could easily spare that amount.

To illustrate the various ways of sending money, Touré opened his wallet and took out a receipt for 25,000 francs, recently sent from Paris by a Malian who had been looking for work. Touré was used to handling large sums of money. He told me, for example, that if it was necessary to wire 1,000,000 francs, it was better to send it in four batches of 250,000.

Touré told us about a Senegalese for whom he had performed maraboutage. As a diplomat in Paris, the man was used to associating with powerful people. He had even met the presidents of the United States and France. Thanks to the "work" that Touré had done for him, the diplomat feared nothing and no one. He had sent Touré 250,000 francs—which the marabout had used to build one of his houses—and told him that he would be glad to send him anything he wanted from France. Touré had taken advantage of his offer only once, requesting a wristwatch, but the diplomat had continued to send him money from time to time anyway.

The two pilgrimages to Mecca made by Touré in the early 1970s had also been paid for by one of his clients. They had traveled together to the Holy City, with Touré's client paying all their expenses.

Boubakar took a last handful of rice. What was left of our meal would be for the garibu who would soon appear at the gate with his begging bowl. The women of the household sat off to one side, talking. The moon, almost full, shone high in the sky. A silvery light illuminated the courtyard. The nicest evenings were those in the middle of the lunar month, when the city's residents stayed up much later than usual. On evenings like these, young girls gathered on street corners to play their dancing games, and groups of boys strolled around the neighborhood. While the old men sat talking for hours at their customary places in front of the houses, their wives and daughters visited one another in the inner courtyards. Sometimes the moonlight was so luminous that the city seemed to be covered with a thin layer of snow.

The meal had made me thirsty. I took several gulps of water. The high-pitched voices of the girls singing songs in front of the neighbor's house had turned, for the umpteenth time, into squeals of laughter. Boubakar took the plastic cup of water from me, and we concluded that marabouts—some of them, at least—could earn a lot of money with maraboutage, though not all of them had the same level of knowledge or achieved the same results. A number of marabouts from Djenné stayed out of town for longer or shorter periods every year, trying to earn money with their knowledge of sirri not only in the surrounding villages, but also in such towns as Mopti and Bamako, and in cities as distant as Abidjan in Ivory Coast, where many migrant workers from Mali went to seek work. Only a few marabouts were famous enough to stay home and work for mail-order clients.

Chapter Eight

*W*hen we took our leave, the marabout—entirely in keeping with the spirit of our visit—pronounced his blessings, "May God help us and you with the work you're doing. May God open your and our minds. May God help you in your writings."

Later that day, when I was working on the notes I'd taken during our talk with the Qur'anic teacher, Boubakar repeated for me the gaara he had recited. In Boubakar's opinion the marabout had expressed himself well, and I asked if he could give me examples of other, similar gaara. Apparently it sufficed to say, "May God bestow baraka on what you do." That was an all-purpose gaara that was good for everything.

Baraka was an important concept. When the subject came up again, I asked Boubakar to explain exactly what it was.

"Baraka gives strength," he replied tersely, and then he launched into a long explanation, which I tried to record as faithfully as possible.

"Baraka gives strength," Boubakar reiterated.

"How can you recognize a person who has baraka?" I asked.

He placed his forearms on the table and leaned forward. "If a person with baraka becomes your enemy, you'll fall in a hole and never get out. When a baraka child finds itself in difficulties, it will be sure to overcome them. A baraka child will always find a way out. It's—"

I stopped him before he could go further. "What's a baraka child?"

"In Songhay we also speak of *nyaa gaara ije*, a child blessed by its mother, and of *baaba gaara ije*, a child blessed by its father. To receive baraka, you must respect others, especially your parents and the elderly. If you respect them, God will respect you too. It's written in the Qur'an, 'Be good to your parents.' After your parents comes your marabout. If you've sought baraka by being good to both your parents and your marabout, if you've received gaara from all of them, you can say you're 'insured.' A child is brought up first by its parents and then by its marabout. It's necessary to put up with a strict upbringing, to obey all commands and observe all prohibitions. Later on, you'll reap the rewards. We have a proverb that says, 'When you honor your own parents, you honor other parents as well.' The gaara you receive from your parents and your marabout offers lifelong protection from calamity. Every time you run into difficulties, God will help you overcome them."

"Can anyone obtain baraka?"

Boubakar nodded. "All good things are given by God, but some people receive more than others. If one person follows his path better than another, that person obtains more baraka. Everyone can receive baraka, even unbelievers, although they receive it only in this life, not in the next.

For everything they do to earn baraka, God rewards them in the here and now, not in the hereafter."

"So what do unbelievers do to earn baraka?"

"They take good care of their parents. They respect them. They take good care of other people. They're hospitable. God will reward them for all of that in this world. But for Muslims it doesn't stop there. They can receive some of their reward in this world and some in the next. Or maybe they'll receive none here and everything later. That's what makes life more difficult for believers. You have to work at acquiring baraka, you have to suffer hardship. Your parents or your marabout can recite gaara for you, but if you don't seek it yourself by dint of hard work, baraka will not be yours, even if someone wishes it for you. It is something you pay for with exhaustion and suffering, with patience and endurance. It's not like buying something in a store and taking it home. If you've sought baraka and received gaara, you might be rewarded sooner or later in this world. And if you're not rewarded here on earth, God will reward you in the next life."

"Can marabouts pass on baraka to others?"

"Yes, of course, because marabouts respect those who were here before them, such as their parents and their marabouts, and because they follow the path of God. The marabouts who follow the path laid down by God and His Prophet are close to God. They are the ones who teach people day in and day out how to read the Qur'an and other important books. They are the ones who see the name of God and His Law in the Qur'an every day. They are the ones who know the difference between good and bad. They are the ones who teach and advise those who are ignorant. Marabouts who do this are important. A pupil seeks gaara and goes on seeking it until his marabout recites gaara for him, after which he is released. These gaara are not easy to come by, but they stay with a person his whole life. A lot of effort goes into getting these gaara, and it is through them that a person receives baraka from God. The marabout asks God to bestow it on his pupil. Each gaara begins with the words 'May God.'"

"Do all marabouts possess baraka?"

"Not necessarily. Some marabouts are very knowledgeable, but don't possess any baraka. The maraboutage they perform may or may not have the desired effect."

While jotting down Boubakar's last remarks, I asked myself what he actually meant by them. At that moment, it seemed like a good time to make coffee, so we moved to the veranda. With a few quick flicks of a wicker fan, Boubakar waved new life into the coals that had been glowing in the brazier since I'd made my morning tea. He threw a handful of charcoal on the fire and put some water on to boil. The flames licked the sides of the kettle.

Boubakar said he felt like a cigarette, and went off to buy one. A bright blue sky could be seen through the arch in the veranda's thick wall. It was bound to be a hot day, but it was still cool on the veranda. While waiting for the water to boil, my thoughts returned to our talk about baraka, and I began thinking about how the subject had come up that morning.

Boubakar had been telling me that he had recently asked Abdoulaye Touré—with whom he had become better acquainted during our frequent visits—to help him with a friend's personal problem. The marabout had given him a "text," that is to say, he had pointed to a specific line in the Qur'an and told Boubakar how his friend could use these words to solve the problem: at a designated time of day that the marabout had determined was favorable, Boubakar's friend was supposed to recite the line from the Qur'an a given number of times and then blow on a bowl of drinking water. By drinking this water, the person could rest assured that the therapeutic powers of the Qur'anic passage would be absorbed by the body.

A few days after receiving the text, Boubakar went to see Touré and brought along some saraa, some *cadeaux*—Boubakar used both terms—which included a can of powdered milk, a large piece of soap, and a few coins, all of which were intended "to increase the baraka of the text he had received from the marabout."

Just as I was pouring boiling water over the Nescafé, Boubakar came up the stairs. We took our coffee to the study. I opened my notebook and read the last few lines I had written. "What was that about marabouts and baraka?" I asked Boubakar. He put his glass down.

"We're talking here about people in general, not about marabouts in particular," he began. "Where baraka is concerned, everyone is involved. Everyone seeks it, but not everyone gets it. Most marabouts have suffered hardship. Some of them worked, while still students, for their parents or their marabout. Many of them worked like slaves for their marabouts. They slept in dirty houses, ate poorly, and wore old clothes. Through the sacrifices they made for their marabouts, they received baraka. The marabout recited gaara for them. Then, in the end, they themselves became marabouts. They will be blessed with good fortune for the rest of their lives. But their fellow pupils, who go on to do other work, will also receive baraka for their exertions and the hardships they suffered, no matter what their vocation is."

Boubakar asked me if I remembered the words of Yousouf Traoré, who had told us not long ago that whenever he went back to his native village, he always spent the first few days with his marabout, and only then did he visit his family. It was his way of seeking baraka. We had also asked Yousouf if he took along saraa for his marabout. Of course he did, he had replied, and every time he heard that someone was going to his village, he gave them something to take to his marabout: tea or sugar or money—whatever he had on hand.

"Baraka is for everyone," Boubakar emphasized again. "The work or vocation in which the baraka manifests itself depends on your destiny, the path you take. If you become a trader and possess a lot of baraka, you will become the biggest and best trader. If you are a marabout and possess a lot of baraka, you will become the most adept at maraboutage."

"Maraboutage?"

"Yes, because marabouts invoke God. If you don't know how to ask God for something, you go to a marabout, because he knows how to do this better than you do. The marabout will ask God to bestow baraka on you. Many things happen in life, and for each thing there is a certain way to ask for God's help."

"Do amulets contain baraka?"

"Yes, all amulets contain baraka. Any time the names or words of God are written on a piece of paper, it's full of baraka. But you have to use such things in the right way. You have to keep them pure and not get them mixed up with things that are bad. You mustn't use amulets to steal, for example, or to cheat or do evil. You must always use them to do good. That way the baraka will stay with you."

"Do you ask a marabout for baraka?"

"Well, I suppose you can look at it that way, because you ask a marabout to help your case by bestowing baraka. But you don't ask the marabout himself for baraka—he's the one who asks it of God. It's okay to give a marabout something in order to receive baraka. You can give him part of your wages, your hard-earned wages. If you give him money that was earned dishonestly—stolen money, for instance—the maraboutage might work, but it won't last long. Whatever baraka was bestowed, even if you profited from it initially, will be used up completely and you'll be left with nothing. In most cases, however, it will have no effect from the very beginning, and you could end up in even bigger trouble. If you are too poor to pay a marabout for his work, you must ask him to do it for the grace of God. That's better than committing theft or fraud."

Boubakar returned to the subject of the text Touré had given him to solve his friend's problem, because he had not only "paid" with saraa to increase the text's baraka, but had also repaired something in the marabout's house. When he arrived at the marabout's with his gifts, he suddenly noticed that the plaster in one of the corners was damaged, and the wall had to be replastered with mud. And since Boubakar was a mason, he was cut out for the job.

The damaged corner had been a sign, Boubakar explained—a sign that God would help him. Touré had not asked him to do the job, and Boubakar had had no way of knowing about the damaged corner until he had decided, on the spur of the moment, to visit Touré. In short, God had shown him a way to help the marabout. "It was a sign that the passage from the Qur'an would have the desired effect, and that God would come to my aid," Boubakar said.

"But you also gave saraa," I remarked. "What did you mean when you said that you gave Touré saraa to increase the baraka in the text?"

"You ask by giving," Boubakar replied. "By giving saraa and having faith in God, by trusting that He will take care of things, you increase the amulet's baraka. The most important thing is to have faith in God and ask Him to hear your prayer. One way to do this is to give saraa to beggars, or to the poor, or to a marabout. If a marabout writes an amulet text for you, you give him saraa. After all, you want to pay him for his work, so you give him saraa and you say, 'I give this to God.' You don't have to say this out loud. You can also say it in your heart. The marabout will then reply, 'May God accept it.' Or he might recite gaara for you. It's up to him to decide what to do."

Around the time of the midday meal a garibu comes to the gate with his begging bowl.

"Do you give saraa to God?"

"Yes, you do give saraa to God. But God needs nothing from us. He has enough of everything. So you give it to a fellow human being. And when a poor person like you gives God something in this way, He will repay you twice over."

*T*he Songhay term saraa is derived from the Arabic *sadaqa*, which means "voluntary alms." Saraa should not be confused with obligatory alms such as the *zakat*, or alms tax, required by the third pillar of Islam. Unlike the payment of zakat, the giving of saraa is not a religious duty. It is a pious act. The Qur'an considers almsgiving to be an extremely praiseworthy deed.

The food offered to garibus, the coins or the handful of grain given to the blind beggar who passes by every Friday, singing songs in praise of the Prophet, the alms given to the two or three blind men who always sit on the stairs to the mosque, and the mutton distributed to neighbors and relatives on the Feast of Sacrifice—all these gifts are saraa. And in every one of these cases, those who are favored with saraa will recite gaara for the giver: anything from the short "May God accept it" quickly mumbled by the garibus to the whole litany of blessings chanted by the beggar for his benefactor.

In October 1989, when I returned to Djenné after a 20-month absence, I acted on Boubakar's advice and offered cadeaux to the imam, the muezzin, and the town chief. We bought dates and kola nuts, and took them to the mosque in the late afternoon. The three dignitaries were seated, as they were almost every day, near the main entrance, where they were conversing with a group of older men while waiting for the fourth prayer of the day. As Boubakar handed them the dates and kola nuts, he explained that these were my saraa and that I was seeking their gaara.

Later, at home, our conversation turned to the topic of saraa. "When you give saraa to someone," Boubakar explained, "regardless of whether it's a marabout or a beggar, you're supposed to say, 'Take this, it is my saraa for you.' That's all you have to say, nothing else. If you want to, you can say to yourself, 'May God let me find what I'm seeking,' though this isn't strictly necessary. The person to whom you give the saraa will recite gaara for you, such as 'May God accept it' or 'May God grant your wish.'"

Saraa are a means of communicating with God. One person gives something to another in the hope that God will grant him or her a special favor in return. The gaara of the recipient functions as a link: he or she asks God to reward the giver. People can decide freely to give saraa as a pious gift, or a marabout can order them to give saraa, as was the case when Boubakar was instructed to give a red chicken and a kola nut in the shape of a horse's head in order to hasten his girlfriend's return.

Marabouts keep lists in which the patterns, letters, and numbers derived from various methods of divination are linked to certain saraa. Sidi Oumar told us that a list giving one or more saraa for each of the 16 "houses" of the turaabu had been compiled by none other than Ali, the Prophet's son-in-law, who had also drawn up a list of saraa that are linked to the various letters of the Arabic alphabet.

One afternoon Sidi and I were examining his copy of this list. Depicted next to the individual letters were such saraa as a loaf of bread, a bowl of cow's milk, ten white kola nuts, an item of clothing, salt, a white chicken, and a red goat. Sidi explained that when a marabout instructs his client to give a specific gift, with the intention of obtaining a certain result, the recipient will ask God to accept the saraa and to grant the giver his wish.

Sometimes a marabout is required to determine precisely which saraa his client should give. Not long after Boubakar's girlfriend had returned to town—much later than the marabouts had predicted—he broke up with her. They had no future together, he felt, if they already had so many problems. In the ensuing weeks, Boubakar was restless, and as he tended to do whenever he was out of sorts, he consulted a marabout. He went to Baber Kontao, who set up the turaabu for him. The outcome was alarming: Boubakar's ex-girlfriend and her family had sought the help of a very powerful marabout and were doing everything they could to get Boubakar to come back to her. The situation was serious, for if the other marabout succeeded, Boubakar would be reunited with his girlfriend, whether he wanted to be or not. To protect himself from the other marabout's machinations, Kontao gave him a bottle of nesi with which to wash himself.

Several days later Boubakar had Baber Kontao read the turaabu again, to see how matters stood. The results were reassuring: the other marabout would succeed only if the family of Boubakar's former girlfriend were to give a particular saraa, but if he couldn't tell them exactly which one was required, his efforts would be in vain. Kontao assured Boubakar that he could keep the marabout from identifying the necessary saraa by washing with the nesi.

Even ordinary, "everyday" saraa—alms given freely, without being prescribed by a marabout—can be instrumental in bringing about a specific result. One day Boubakar asked if he could have the next morning off to visit a relative in a nearby village—a "grandfather" (actually his maternal grandfather's brother) we had previously visited together. On that occasion the old man had shown us his "book of dreams." Boubakar had had a dream about black snakes, which had upset him, and now he wanted to consult the book to find out what the dream meant.

The old, handwritten sheaves of paper that comprised the book of dreams contained a long list of subjects. It could be consulted to determine the message of a dream in which someone saw a sheep, water, lots of women, or indeed dozens of other things, such as lions, black birds, blood, and rain. Each theme was accompanied by three things: the dream's meaning or message, a saraa, and a Qur'anic text. To hasten the advent of the favors forecast by the dream, or to ward off the evil it portended, the dreamer had to give the prescribed saraa and wash with nesi in which the relevant Qur'anic passage had been dissolved.

When Boubakar got back he told me that, according to his grandfather's book, a dream about snakes—not necessarily black ones, since the book did not go into such detail—meant that one would have a long life and many offspring, mainly sons. That was not in the least alarming. The book had also told him which saraa and which Qur'anic text were linked to snake dreams.

We talked about this again the next day. Boubakar had meanwhile given the requisite saraa to his sister. He had also made nesi from the prescribed Qur'anic text and had washed with it. He had done this to make sure that the positive things the dream augured would really come true. I asked him what would have happened if he hadn't consulted the book of dreams and therefore hadn't known what needed to be done.

Boubakar's answer was surprising. In order to make a dream come true or to avert the danger or evil it predicted, it was not strictly necessary to give the saraa listed in the book of dreams. After all, it wasn't as though you consulted a marabout about every dream you had. He had gone to see his grandfather only because he had been alarmed by the snake images. But even if he hadn't asked for advice and hadn't known what the dream meant or what he should do about it, it would not necessarily have an adverse effect on the happy prospect held out by the dream, since he regularly gave alms—"as our religion requires"—to a beggar or a needy person, and each time he did so, the recipient recited a gaara, asking God to reward him. In the case at hand, even if Boubakar had remained ignorant of the meaning of his dream, the gaara would ensure that the good fortune betokened by a snake dream could come true.

Saraa are expressions of a person's search for spiritual and material well-being. These pious gifts, the giving of which is praiseworthy but not compulsory, belong to the public domain of bayaanu knowledge, yet saraa can also serve a purely personal and worldly purpose. In this respect they are similar to written amulets, which are typical products of sirri practice. Boubakar's explanation showed how close the domains of sirri and bayaanu can be. The bestowal of a pious gift recommended by a religious precept does not differ in essence from the bestowal of a gift prescribed by a marabout to achieve a specific goal. In the former case, the goal—even if formulated less precisely—may also be the attainment of a divine reward in the here and now.

*T*he following is one of the many statements Boubakar made that I recorded in my notebook: "Marabouts teach us how to follow God, and marabouts know how to invoke God." This is a concise definition of the two forms of knowledge marabouts possess. While "teaching us how to follow God" expresses the essence of the bayaanu domain, "knowing how to invoke God" characterizes the sirri domain. What marabouts do is "invoke God." The "praying" referred to by the man from Bamako who wrote to Abdoulaye Touré involved the recitation of gaara, or petitionary prayers. Marabouts petition God to protect their clients, to cure them, to let them prosper, to make their wishes come true.

The Qur'an occupies a central position in both the bayaanu and sirri domains, since God's Word contains not only His message to believers but also beneficent powers. Even before a pupil at a Qur'anic school learns how to pronounce the first words of the Holy Book, he absorbs God's words by licking off the palm of his right hand the Qur'anic passage written there by his teacher, thus assimilating the powers contained in those words. In this way God is asked to "open" the pupil's mind. The baraka in Qur'anic words, which is such an important part of sirri practice, is used to further the task of the bayaanu marabout, namely to pass on the knowledge needed to function as a member of Muslim society.

Both amulet-making and divination are activities whose legitimacy has traditionally been a point of discussion among Muslims. Orthodox norms are at issue here, but amulets can also be considered a way of "invoking God," and it is this characterization of amulets as petitionary prayers that lends them legitimacy. Support for this viewpoint can be found in the bayaanu domain: in the knowledge of the Qur'an and the traditions of the Prophet. After all, it is written in the Qur'an, "Call upon me and I shall answer you" (40:60), while the Prophet stated in the hadîth that "petitionary prayers are the weapons of the Muslim." These were the two texts quoted by the marabouts in Djenné during our discussions of the use and production of amulets.

Divination—the other practice characteristic of the sirri domain— also contains an element of ambivalence. Classical scholars have commented at length on this subject as well. Knowledge of secret things and of the future belongs to God, and man should steer clear of such matters. But as Abdoulaye Touré once told me when we were talking about various ways to predict the future, "People do what is frowned upon."

Here too, however, there is a mechanism that provides a link to the respected domain of bayaanu. Predictions of the future are often tied to the compulsory giving of saraa—the almsgiving defined by Islam as pious. In the case of new year's tidings, such predictions are firmly rooted in the tradition of almsgiving and petitionary prayer. The important thing, as Hamidou Sanogo once noted, is that these predictions prompt a person to give saraa and to ask God for protection by means of gaara.

The domains of bayaanu and sirri both play a role in the definition of concepts associated with gaara and saraa. Concepts whose religious meaning is defined in the bayaanu domain also have a place in the sirri domain. There is a "public" as well as a "secret" side to petitionary prayer and almsgiving. Elements from the sirri domain can be legitimized to some extent by providing them with clear links to the respected domain of bayaanu.

However, defining amulets as gaara and blurring the boundary between saraa rooted in one domain or the other is not the only way to lend sirri matters respectability: it is also possible to place the origin of certain sirri knowledge within the historical framework of Islam. For example, the source of the turaabu can be traced back to the prophet Idris, who received knowledge of this divination technique in a divine revelation. Furthermore, Ali, Muhammad's son-in-law—who is said to have "known everything about maraboutage"—is considered to be the compiler of a list of saraa, tied to the use of the Qur'an as an instrument of divination, as well as the discoverer of God's "greatest name," which plays such an important role in amulet texts. Moreover, legend has it that Muhammad and earlier prophets saved themselves in perilous circumstances with the help of "texts" revealed to them by God. Sirri knowledge is thus endowed with an acceptable, historical context, which is closely linked to the lives of Islam's leaders and prophets.

*A*s Abdoulaye Touré explained, the lives of each and every one of us are recorded on the "well-preserved tablet" that is kept in heaven. But, he added, the things that can happen to a person are of three kinds: first, there are things that simply happen to us, which we are powerless to prevent; second, there are things that can be achieved by asking for them, by reciting gaara; and third, there are things that can be achieved or acquired by giving saraa. Touré thus revealed the significance of a marabout's knowledge, because when a person must ask for some things and give alms for others, it is important to know how to ask and what to give. It is this knowledge in which Touré and other marabouts specialize.

Boubakar once told me about the end of time. It was a theme that cropped up occasionally in our talks, just as we sometimes talked about

Paradise, particularly after a visit to a marabout who had brought up the subject. After all, earthly existence is full of suffering, and one serves God in order to be free of cares in the life to come. The prospect of a reward in the hereafter makes the trials and tribulations of life on earth bearable, for the Day of Reckoning will come, and each person's book of deeds will be opened and each person will be judged.

Before the Final Judgment, however, a number of omens will reveal that the end is at hand. Boubakar had heard from the "old men" what would happen. "When the end of time is drawing near, goodness will disappear from the face of the earth. People will turn their backs on religion and ignore the precepts of Islam. To keep them from abusing the Qur'an or not treating it seriously enough, the angels will take every copy of the Holy Book up to heaven. At the end, all goodness will be gone from the earth, and only evil will remain. There won't be any marabouts either. Eventually they—and their knowledge—will disappear, until it will be impossible to find anyone with a marabout's wisdom. If you do happen to hear of a marabout who is still alive, it will be a long time before you hear of another one. There will be fewer and fewer of them until not one remains. When the end of time finally arrives, there won't be a single marabout left on earth."

The author, working with his assistant, Boubakar Kouroumansé, on his fieldwork notes (July 1987).

Sand and Time

To give Alfa Baba Kampo an impression of the Netherlands, I had brought along a few calendar pictures. We looked at the photographs of green pastures full of cows with gleaming udders—"Do the cows in your country really give so much milk?"—of wide rivers flowing slowly through endless lowlands, of the Delta Works—"Oh, those white people know how to work!"—and of step-gabled houses in Amsterdam. The marabout looked intently at the pictures.

We had talked about the Netherlands once before. On that occasion Kampo had told us that he sometimes listened to a program in Arabic broadcast by Radio Netherlands Worldwide. This had prompted him to ask me if there were any Muslims in my country, and any mosques, and whether we ate pork.

While Boubakar translated for me, I tried to think of the best way to explain what my country was like. Although I routinely asked other people about their culture, I now noticed—not for the first time—how difficult it was to tell them something about my own background. The Netherlands was far away, and those calendar pictures did not tell the whole story. Besides that, I knew very little about some of the things they did illustrate. How many liters of milk *do* Dutch cows give a day?

Suddenly we heard a noise outside. Kampo laid down a photo of a tulip field in riotous bloom, spun around on his mat, and opened the outside door a bit more. We could hear voices calling out with great urgency. The marabout craned his neck to see out into the street. I thought I caught the word *baana*, but wasn't sure, because—as I knew from the lists of Songhay words I'd learned by heart—baana meant rain. That couldn't be right.

Rain was something from the world of the calendar pictures we were looking at. I hadn't seen or felt a drop of rain in six months. My memory

131

of wetter climes had been burned away by the scorching heat of the sun. Not only that, but this was April, which meant that the rainy season in this part of the Sahel wasn't due to begin for another six weeks—assuming there would be one, since very little rain had fallen these last few years. "Only God knows if this year will be better" was an oft-heard refrain. At any rate, I'd never known this mud-brick city as anything other than hot and dusty.

Kampo said something to Boubakar, and this time I was sure they were talking about baana. Kampo's remark seemed to make Boubakar nervous; he said we had to get moving. At first I assumed that he wanted us to move from the vestibule into the house, but then he told me we had to go home immediately. I gathered up the calendar pictures, put them in my bag, together with my pen and notebook, and shook Kampo's hand. Boubakar was already outside, ready to jump on his bicycle.

Outdoors the light was eerie. In the east the sky was overcast, and a thick yellowy fog seemed to hang in the air. It was clear from Boubakar's behavior that we had no time to lose. He jumped on his bicycle and I followed suit, still surprised at the suddenness of it all.

The streets were deserted. Everyone had taken refuge behind the thick mud walls of their houses. Even before we reached the end of Kampo's narrow street, the sand caught up with us. Suddenly everything was yellow, and sand was whirling everywhere, covering us from head to foot. Visibility was less than two meters. Boubakar's bicycle zigzagged in front of me. Sand forced its way into my eyes, ears, nose, and mouth. The wind blew savagely, and we were lashed by sand. A magical kaleidoscope appeared before my eyes, as the sand cloud seemed to flash past in layer after layer of brightly colored hues: orange, yellow, red, and all their combinations. For a few seconds it was pitch dark and I could see nothing at all. I sensed that we were in the middle of the market square. I called out to Boubakar. A hellish flash of light cut through the cloud. Squinting to keep the sand out of my eyes, I could see that we were bicycling on the north side of the mosque, which meant we'd already crossed the square. "Watch out! A donkey!" Boubakar cried, as I just missed hitting the grayish lump pressed against a wall. The sand whipped past us in orange and yellow gusts. I could just make out the contours of the houses lining the narrow streets. Boubakar shouted out to me, to make sure I was still there. I yelled that I was following him, then quickly shut my mouth again. Sand grated between my teeth.

Suddenly, after I had lost all notion of how much distance we'd covered, we appeared to have reached my house. We dropped our bicycles in the courtyard and ran upstairs. Sand was blowing around the veranda. While Boubakar closed the shutters in my study, I closed the door and lit

Djenné after a downpour.

the lamp. The wind howled around the house, rattling the shutters and tugging at the corrugated-iron doors. I spit out sand, rubbed it out of my eyes, and blew it out of my nose. Boubakar and I shared what little lemonade I had to rinse the sand out of our throats. In the lamplight Boubakar's hair and face, which were covered with a fine layer of sand, looked gray. I couldn't hide my amazement at the sight.

Ten minutes later we heard the patter of rain. Boubakar opened one of the shutters. "Isn't this nice!" he exclaimed. I opened the door. After months of heat, the cool air streaming in was more than welcome. Rain beat down on the city. The drops bouncing off the newly plastered roof of the house across the street looked like hailstones. In the lane visible from the window, the initial trickle of water quickly turned into a torrent. Jets of dirty rainwater, mixed with the upper layer of the mud roofs, gushed from the ceramic pipes projecting from the rooflines.

When the rain let up a bit, I went out on the roof, armed with an umbrella, to have a look. Below, children were bursting out of doorways and running through the puddles, whooping with glee. Then all at once the rain stopped, having lasted no more than about fifteen minutes. Boubakar rushed home to make sure everything was okay. By now every child in the neighborhood had come outside and was running around boisterously. The mud squelched beneath their bare feet. I gazed upon a city that had just had a drenching: the houses were sodden and the streets ran with mud. The rain had turned the three towers of the mosque a different color. In the distant plain, huge puddles of water glistened in the sunlight breaking through the clouds. People were walking around on their roofs, assessing the damage caused by the pounding rain. Here and there someone stopped to fill in a hole with mud. The air was startlingly fresh.

As Boubakar and I ate supper I compared the natural phenomenon that had caught us unawares that afternoon to the end of time. Boubakar chuckled at this, and related what I'd said to the women, who were seated around their own dish of fish and rice in the courtyard. They laughed heartily, and told stories about the times they had been surprised by much worse sandstorms in the bush.

$\mathcal{L}$ater on, when the season came, I witnessed several more sandstorms, but never again did I experience it in quite the same way as that first time. A few years ago a Dutch newspaper printed an article on the rich history of Segou, Djenné, and Timbuktu titled "The Stories Lie Beneath the Sand." The accompanying illustration was a photograph of Djenné's Great Mosque. My fieldwork has long since turned into deskwork, but I am regularly reminded of that storm with its lashing and all-enveloping sand. At the same time, I am all too aware that the Djenné I got to know in the late 1980s has disappeared beneath the sand of time.

To be sure, the past decade has seen a number of changes. Several of the marabouts who were very important to my fieldwork have died, and Boubakar's grandmother and both his parents have passed away as well. Meanwhile, Boubakar has become the head of a family. In 1990 he married Aminata Niafo, and they now have three children: a son and two daughters. To accommodate them, Boubakar tore down his parents' house and built a new and bigger one in its place.

The rest of the city has also changed. Since the mid-1980s, the infrastructure has been modernized to some extent. First the rusty, rickety float that used to ferry people across the Bani River was replaced by a motorized ferry. Then the old first-aid station disappeared and a hospital—much larger and better equipped—was opened. Finally, a public-address system was installed in the mosque, so that the call to prayer could be broadcast over the city five times a day.

In July 1994, when I last visited Djenné, the final leg of my journey was much smoother than it used to be. The narrow dike, which had been notorious for its potholes, had been widened and paved with asphalt, and the road running from the river bank to the outskirts of the city had also been paved. Another surprise that year was the change in Djenné's roofscape: a number of houses boasted a bamboo pole crowned with a TV antenna. At that time Djenné's few television owners still had to have their own power supply, but Boubakar wrote to me in August 1996 to let me know that the city had been electrified. Friends and colleagues who have recently visited Djenné tell of streetlights, brightly lit houses, and television sets glowing in courtyards. I find it hard to imagine.

Another sign of modernization is the increase in the number of houses with running water and, to a lesser extent, a hookup to the telephone network. Yet at the same time some parts of the city are falling into disrepair at a truly frightening pace. The maintenance of many of the mud-brick houses is inadequate or nonexistent, and the fragile adobe structures are decaying at an alarming rate. Each rainy season produces several new ruins.

The Dutch National Museum of Ethnology in Leiden recently set up a long-term restoration project to protect Djenné's cultural heritage. For the benefit of the Malian partners and project leaders, an office has been set up in Djenné and furnished with modern computers. An Internet connection is also planned. Soon I'll be able to communicate with Boubakar, who is working for the project, via the information superhighway.

Djenné in 2007

$\mathcal{I}$n the epilogue, written more than ten years ago, I mentioned a number of changes that had occurred in Djenné between the mid-1980s and mid-1990s. Now that more than another decade has passed and Djenné's progression—or rather giant leap—toward modernity has become even more noticeable, the time has come to update my portrayal of the city. I last visited Djenné in October–November 2007. The following collage is based on the journal I kept at the time.

18 October 2007. The sound of a stern male voice, distorted by a loudspeaker, brings back memories. Boubakar and I are sitting on the roof of his house. Earlier this evening Nan and I arrived for a two-week stay in Djenné. Nan is sitting downstairs in the courtyard with Aminata and the girls. Boubakar's oldest daughters—Bajolie (13) and Gogo (12)—are helping their mother prepare supper. Four-year-old Aya is flitting around the courtyard. The two sons, Ba Komor (16) and Elhadji (8), are sitting with us on the roof. The city lies all around us. Here and there the façades of the houses are illuminated by the glow of fluorescent lights. The silhouette of the mosque stands out darkly against the light from the lampposts in the market square. The amplified voice drifts over to us from the left. Ba Komor explains that we're hearing a sermon (waaju), marking the end of the tafsîr readings, given by a marabout in the neighborhood of the post office. This evening is the last in a series of gatherings—at which the Qur'an and an exegetical commentary are read aloud—held to mark Ramadan, the month of fasting that ended less than a week ago. Over the last few days, other marabouts at other places in town have already concluded their tafsîr. These gatherings are held on successive days, to give as many people as possible an opportunity to attend them.

The world was 265 moons younger when I took part in Ramadan in Djenné, and Boubakar and I had attended a tafsîr gathering nearly every day. Twenty-three months of fasting have gone by since then. Boubakar is 21 years older now and so am I.

Suddenly the sermon is drowned out by the crackle of a loudspeaker being turned on nearby. Immediately afterward, a number of highly amplified voices begin the rhythmical recitation of the Arabic formula *la ilaha il Allah* ("There is no god but God"). This is new. I've never heard it broadcast before. Surprised, I ask Boubakar what is going on. "It's Tijanis with their *wirdi*," he says curtly, meaning members of the Tijaniyya Sufi brotherhood performing the recitations prescribed by their order (Arabic: *wird*). I ask Boubakar if they've been doing this for a long time. He says he doesn't know exactly when they began, because he was out of town at the time, but it's a fairly recent development. He's clearly reluctant to say anything more about it. While playing with his new cell phone, he adds, "They're crazy. They annoy the whole neighborhood, and a lot of people have complained about them."

Every day of our stay in Djenné—at least when we're at Boubakar's house—we're startled by the amplified wirdi marking the times of the five daily prayers. Especially at 5:30 AM, when we're forced to listen to the blaring voices—one or two of which invariably sing out of tune, declaring 50 times in a row that God is the only god—I think back nostalgically to the Djenné of 20 years ago, where one woke up in the morning to the sound of braying donkeys and crowing roosters, and women bustling around as they went about their household chores. Although mystic brotherhoods have been in the city for a long, long time, they played no role in public life when I was doing my fieldwork in Djenné. Only in answer to our questions did marabouts tell us whether they belonged to the Tijaniyya or the Qadiriyya brotherhood, or none at all. A few members explained in general terms the difference between the two brotherhoods: the Qadiriyya do not recite their wirdi collectively, whereas the Tijaniyya gather in the mosque to recite their wirdi around 5:00 AM, after the *al-fajr* prayer, and at the end of the day on Friday, after the *salât al-magrib*. I never witnessed such a gathering, however. In fact, the subject of the brotherhoods seldom came up, which is why the Tijaniyya and Qadiriyya were allotted very little space in my fieldwork notes.

I suddenly hear music—an English pop song—coming from the vicinity of Boubakar's chair. He stretches out his arm and, beaming with obvious pleasure, shows me his Samsung SGH D840. On its screen is a clip with a blonde singer: Celine Dion, Boubakar informs me. We listen for a minute, then Boubakar taps a few buttons, and now his cell phone is blaring Malian music. A new band, he explains. But before the song can come to an end, Boubakar punches some more buttons and suddenly we're listening to a recitation from the Qur'an. Again Boubakar holds the phone in front of my face. *Ayat al-Kursi* (The Throne Verse), he says, and chants along as the voice in the phone recites this important verse. He's also recorded the Ya Sin sura, he says. He starts searching for it, so that I can hear it too, but before he finds it, we hear the opening chords of a "desert blues" number performed by the famous Malian guitarist and singer Ali Farka Touré. This is Boubakar's ring tone—a sound I'll hear repeatedly in the next two weeks.

While Boubakar talks on the phone, Nan joins us on the roof and announces that supper is almost ready. A short while later Aminata appears at the top of the stairs with a platter of food in her hands. She's followed by Bajolie, who carries the jug of drinking water, and Gogo, who carries a basin of water for us to wash our hands. Once they've placed everything before us, mother and daughters go back downstairs to have their evening meal in the courtyard. Before uncovering the food, Boubakar tucks his phone into his breast pocket.

21 October 2007. Boubakar and I were talking when he suddenly dashed into his bedroom and came back with a catalogue from a museum in the South Korean city of Gimhae. Leafing through it, I was surprised to see my name. At the back of the catalogue, in a biographical sketch of Boubakar, I read the following: "From 1985 to 1987 he started to work with Dutch anthropologist Geert Mommersteeg (author of *In the City of the Marabouts*)."

Boubakar fetched the catalogue because I'd asked about his trip to South Korea, where he and five other masons from Djenné went last spring to participate in the exhibition *Adobe Mosques*, held at the Clayarch Gimhae Museum. As master mason, he was in charge of building a model of a mosque seven meters square and four meters high, to grace the museum's central hall. I told him that I had followed the entire process from the Netherlands by looking at the weekly updates posted on the Internet. Boubakar then took out his digital camera and showed me the photos he'd taken, as well as several short films he'd made in South Korea.

According to Boubakar's biographical sketch in the catalogue, his trip to South Korea was not the first time he had traveled abroad to display his skill and knowledge of traditional masonry. In 1988 he had been invited by a number of friends to spend three months in the Netherlands. Some of this time was spent at the Eindhoven University of Technology, where he made clay models depicting the architectural style typical of Djenné. In both 2003 and 2004 he traveled to France to give demonstrations of Djenné masonry in Angers and Bourgogne. Also in 2003 he was part of the large delegation from Mali that attended the Smithsonian Folklife Festival in Washington, DC, where—on the Mall, within sight of the Capitol—he and several other Djenné masons made an almost life-size replica of the gateway to Djenné.

Toward the end of my stay, Boubakar and I will make a few trips to the Internet Point on the northwest edge of town to send e-mails to the Delft University of Technology in the Netherlands, where a conference devoted to African architecture and urban development, African Perspectives/Perspectives Africaines, will take place at the beginning of December. Boubakar and his team—three of the masons who traveled with him to South Korea—have been invited, as part of the "built heritage" program, to construct large models in Dutch clay of two Djenné-style façades: one representing a house and the other a mosque.

23 October 2007. Yousouf Traoré has obviously changed clothes for the occasion. When Boubakar phoned him half an hour ago to ask if we could drop by, Yousouf said that he'd just come in from his field, where he'd begun harvesting the sorghum. But he was happy to hear that I was in town and said that we were welcome to visit. Boubakar and I had drawn up a list of the people I wanted to see, and Yousouf was one of them. There had been no time to visit this marabout, with whom I had shared a house for so long, on my last two trips to Djenné, both of which had been rather brief.

Yousouf receives us in his neat blue boubou and snow-white skullcap, and we sit down on mats in a corner of the spacious courtyard, which accommodates a few simple dwellings on its periphery. Yousouf's heavily pregnant wife and two of his children are sitting nearby. We exchange greetings. Again Yousouf grips my hand, laughs heartily, and tells me how happy he is to see me. His friendly face is framed by a short gray beard, and the hair escaping from under his skullcap is gray as well. When I remark on this, Yousouf says that my hair has gone gray too. "Not only gray," I add, "but thinner too." We inquire after the children. Yousouf and his wife now have five offspring—including a set of twins— and a sixth is due to arrive shortly. The triplets, whose birth followed that of their oldest son, did not live long.

Three years ago Yousouf and his family moved back to Djenné. Before that they had lived for two years in his native village, some two hundred kilometers north of Djenné, where Yousouf had spent a season working on the land of his marabout, the man who had taught him as a child. All he had been allowed to do was fertilize the fields with manure. The small house he currently lives in is the first house he's ever paid rent on. After being forced to leave the house we shared because the landlord had other plans for it, he lived in three other houses that were put at his disposal "by the grace of God."

I ask Yousouf if he still has pupils. Yes, a number of older talibés study with him, but at the moment they're back in their villages, working in the fields. He himself no longer studies with a marabout. His teacher, Allaye Diallo, died about ten years ago, and when Diallo's son took over his father's school, he wasn't nearly at Yousouf's "level."

How is Saadou? Just asking that question conjures up images of Saadou's tearful Qur'an recitations. On previous visits I'd occasionally run into Saadou at the market, where he did a little business. Yousouf tells me that Saadou has returned to his village. "He's old enough to marry," he adds. But his wife informs us that meanwhile Saadou has married his older brother's widow. I ask after Mamadou, the little Dogon boy who used to live with us. Does Yousouf have any news of him? It takes a minute for Yousouf to realize who Mamadou is. When he finally remembers, he says that the boy was not his pupil; Mamadou had been taught by one of his older pupils. Apparently Mamadou and his teacher left the city a long time ago.

Boubakar asks if Yousouf's children attend the French school. "The oldest do," he says. "School is a necessity these days." Boubakar concurs wholeheartedly, and says that all his children go to school, except little Aya, who will soon start kindergarten.

There are clear signs in Djenné that more and more parents have come to realize the importance of French education. In the 1980s and 1990s the city had two state schools, one of which was Franco-Arabic (in which the curriculum of the *école fondamentale* was supplemented with several hours a week of Arabic). But recently two large schools have been built on the west and east sides of town. The level of secular education offered to children in Djenné has risen considerably in the past few years.

26 October 2007. It's Friday afternoon—almost time for the midday prayer. The la ilaha il Allah can be heard in the room where we've just eaten our noon meal. Unamplified, for once, and gradually coming closer. I turn around on the large couch—which, together with three matching armchairs, takes up a substantial part of Boubakar's small living room—kneel on the fat cushions, and stick my head out the window. In the street below I see six men and a couple of boys singing as they walk by. They're dressed in white robes and turbans. Boubakar remains seated. I turn to him and say that they're all wearing handsome turbans. "Oh, very nice," he says scornfully, "so they've got turbans! I'll be going to the mosque dressed like this," and he pointed to the jeans, T-shirt, and denim jacket he had on. "Clothes don't matter in Islam," he informs me. "The heart does," he adds sternly. Even at the Kaaba in Mecca there are people who pray like this, dressed in their everyday clothes, just as he is now. He saw this on the Saudi Arabian channel. He'll show me some time on his satellite TV.

Still upset by the group that had just walked past, Boubakar says—getting more irritated by the minute—that he knows what those people are like, and he knows his religion. The Qur'an contains a sura about such people: the *al-Munafiqun* (The Hypocrites) sura. It's about people who pose as Muslims but aren't true Muslims. "Haïdara has spoken about this too," he added.

A short while later, after Boubakar has performed his ritual washing (*wudhu*), I see him leave the house, prayer beads in hand, wearing his jeans and denim jacket. How different from those other Friday afternoons, when he used to put on his best boubou to go to the mosque for the most important prayer of the week. I decide to return to the subject of the al-Munafiqun sura and especially the famous Malian preacher Cherif Ousmane Madani Haïdara.

27 October 2007. "As the world grows older, all kinds of new things appear," I read in my notebook. The past few days we've visited several marabouts and asked them what has changed in Djenné since I first visited the city in the mid-1980s. "Was there running water then?" "Was there electricity?" "Were there many televisions in the city?" they asked. In addition to these "novelties that make life easier," they mentioned the new laterite road on the northwest side of the city, and the fact that the population has increased in the last two decades. Not only has the older Kanafa Quarter on the west side of the city grown, but two new quarters have sprung up in the east, on the other side of the access bridge. One or two people have mentioned the dam in the Bani River near Talo, 150 kilometers upriver, which sparked fierce protest when it was built. They still don't know what effect it will have on water levels in the floodplains around Djenné. There's enough water this year at any rate. It promises to be a good fishing season.

Now, after our stroll through town this morning, I go over my notes and am surprised, yet again, that whenever I broached the subject of change, no one ever pointed out that the city is not only larger and more modern, but also much dirtier. The only exception was Amadou Tahirou Bah, whom we met a week ago, but that's hardly surprising, since this educational consultant and former teacher is one of the founding directors of Djenné Patrimoine, the association established in 1995 to promote and protect Djenné's cultural heritage. I don't have to consult my notes in this case; I remember his words perfectly. When I remarked that Djenné had changed considerably, he replied, "Yes, a lot has changed, but the worst thing is the pollution." Unable to hide his frustration, he added, "Our leaders couldn't care less about cleaning it up! It's the last thing on their minds!"

Although in recent years international agencies have financed various projects aimed at improving such things as the drainage of wastewater, every walk through the city proves Bah's point. In many places pollution is a big problem, a blight on the urban landscape.

The problem is twofold: the disposal of both wastewater and "modern" household refuse in a city that has neither a sewage nor a waste-processing system. Fifteen years ago, when I bought a loaf of bread, it was usually wrapped in a scrap of used paper or cardboard. Now, however, it comes in a plastic bag, and if I buy two loaves, I get two plastic bags, and more often than not a handy plastic carrier bag as well. And all that plastic ends up somewhere in the city, much of it scattered around the outskirts. From whichever direction one approaches Djenné, the sight of the city is marred by an embankment littered with plastic. A mud town rising up from a dump.

In the past, city dwellers had to fetch water from public taps and store it in earthenware jars, but now most houses have running water, which has resulted in a huge increase in consumption. In recent years more than 1,100 homes—approximately two-thirds of all the houses in the city—have been hooked up to an infiltration system that channels the wastewater from each house to a concrete cesspit and into a gravel filtration bed. In addition, about thirty houses are connected to so-called *mini-égouts*—underground PVC pipes that carry the water to the outskirts of the city—and the larger streets and a few smaller ones have concrete gutters that likewise disgorge wastewater outside the city. But all of these systems require maintenance, which is often woefully inadequate. As the head of the Department of Sanitation and Pollution Control of Djenné wrote this spring in *Djenné Patrimoine Informations,* "No technical solution will have the expected results without the cooperation of the residents: the most important thing is to change patterns of individual behavior with regard to waste disposal."

These days, anyone exploring the streets and alleyways of Djenné is forced in many places to walk cautiously alongside stinking gutters clogged with plastic and other refuse, to negotiate muddy pools next to blocked cesspits, and to skirt around puddles of scummy green water teeming with clouds of mosquitoes.

The pollution also affects tourism, which has recently become one of the city's most important sources of income. More than 15,000 tourists visit Djenné every year. The simple Hotel-Campement, where I spent my first night in the city in October 1985, now competes with half a dozen hotels, which offer facilities ranging from basic accommodation for backpackers to the air-conditioned rooms demanded by many tourists nowadays. The old Hotel-Campement has managed to improve its quality rating in recent years by carrying out a number of renovations. Even though the city, with its fascinating adobe architecture and colorful Monday market, still advertises itself as "the jewel of the Niger Valley," tourists post blogs voicing their complaints about the filthy conditions they encountered there. It would be difficult to find a description more concise or accurate than the one given by an English tourist who posted his short film about Djenné on YouTube, along with his verdict: "a beautiful dirty spellbinding town."

28 October 2007. Boubakar and the marabout Bokary Kebe, listening to a recitation of the Ya Sin sura that Boubakar downloaded to his new cell phone.

30 October 2007. Laughing amiably, his head covered by a red-and-white checked *keffiyeh*, and flanked by portraits of the members of the central office and the chairmen of the local branches of Ançar Dine, the face of the spiritual leader Haïdara gazes down at us from the poster. The calendar that Boubakar has hanging next to this poster also boasts the face of Haïdara.

Cherif Ousmane Madani Haïdara is the head of Ançar Dine (literally, the helpers of the religion), the best-known and most successful of the various Islamic groupings that sprang up following the democratization of Mali in 1991. In his sermons, recorded on audiocassettes and distributed from Bamako since the mid-1980s, Haïdara emphasizes the importance of personal devotion and ethical behavior, which distinguishes "true believers" from those who merely pretend to believe—in other words, the hypocrites. It is people's deeds that make them good Muslims, not their knowledge of Islamic doctrine. Haïdara lashes out against injustice and corruption, and continually stresses the importance of Islamic precepts in daily life. His rhetorical gifts are highly praised, and his sermons have been recorded on countless audio- and videocassettes by Ançar Dine and circulated among its members. His charismatic voice can be heard every Friday morning on Radio Jamana—Djenné's local station. Both Haïdara's movement and his personal popularity are still growing, not only in Mali but in the whole of West Africa, and also among Malian migrants in Europe and the United States. The *maouloud* gatherings that mark the birthday and name day of the Prophet, which Ançar Dine has held in Bamako's sports stadium in recent years, attract tens of thousands of visitors.

Seated next to the portraits of his favorite preacher, I ask Boubakar to return to the subject of the sura he mentioned last Friday when the Tijanis passed his house on their way to the mosque. I don't learn very much about sura 63—the al-Munafiqun sura—other than that it speaks, as its title suggests, of hypocrites, and that Haïdara gives a detailed commentary on this sura in a sermon of which Boubakar has a recording. However, the question prompts Boubakar to hold forth on the subject of his Ançar Dine membership and how important it is to him. A member since 1991, he journeyed to Bamako to hand over to Haïdara personally the "founding document of the Ançar association of Djenné." At one time he even served as treasurer of the Djenné branch. He tells me again about the difficult period following the death of his parents (who both died in 1989): how often he listened to Haïdara's sermons and how much comfort they gave him. In the meantime he's collected a large number of these cassettes. Recently, during Ramadan, he frequently sat up here on the roof and listened to Haïdara in the peace and quiet of the night.

On all my visits to Djenné from the early 1990s onward, Boubakar has brought up the subject of his membership in Ançar Dine. He has repeatedly told me—in what have sometimes turned into long and fiery monologues—how much his religion means to him and how Islam has been such an important guide in his life, and he never fails to mention Haïdara and his association.

31 October 2007. Around 12:30 PM Dicko—Boubakar's second wife— brings in the bowls containing our meal. Today and tomorrow it's her turn to cook. This also means that Boubakar will spend tonight and tomorrow night at her place. When they married in 2005, he rented an apartment for her a few doors down from his house. Every two days, Aminata and Dicko exchange wifely duties.

After we finish our rice and fish, I leaf through my papers in search of my list of marabouts. Almost every time I come to Djenné, Boubakar and I go through the list of the 40 Qur'anic schools we visited in 1986–87, and every time I have to write "deceased" after a few more names: three-fourths of the marabouts we spoke to at those schools have since died. The schools themselves still exist, however. The teaching duties have been taken over by the following generation, in most cases a son or nephew, many of whom spent years teaching beside their fathers or uncles. Bouba-kar isn't sure about one of the names I mention; perhaps the school no longer exists. He says we'll have to ask someone who knows.

We finish going through the list, and just as I'm making a note to remind myself to inquire about that school, Boubakar whips out his cell phone, scrolls through his list of contacts, and places a call. He briefly greets the person at the other end of the line, then asks about the fate of the school we'd just been talking about. A moment later he switches off his phone and delivers the news: "The school still exists." Nowadays an anthropologist in Djenné can acquire information very quickly indeed. Sometimes all it takes is one phone call.

It is interesting to see that Boubakar has taken to the cell phone with a vengeance. A couple of days ago I asked him how many numbers he had in his list of contacts. While he scrolled through his list, counting five names at a time, I kept score in the margin of my notebook until we came to a grand total of 320 names. But as Boubakar hastened to point out, he had more than 100 numbers in his old phone that still had to be transferred to his new directory.

3 November 2007. It's my last evening bath here—tomorrow we'll be leaving for Bamako and flying back to the Netherlands from there—and while scooping water out of the bucket with a plastic cup and pouring it over myself, I make two mental lists: (1) rice husks, straw, pebbles, a mango pit, peanut shells, pieces of scallop, splinters of charcoal, a candy wrapper, and the silver foil from a package of cigarettes; (2) see-through plastic, blue plastic, black plastic, a plastic pen cap, a plastic medicine strip, and plasticized paper. I make a mental note above the first list, "old," and above the second, "new." I resolve to record the lists in my notebook later that evening.

This past week, while drying myself off after my morning and evening baths, I've been scrutinizing the layer of mud plaster covering the wall of the bathroom. Modern-day refuse is creeping into the very fabric of the houses.

*B*etween 1996 and 2004, 100 monumental houses in Djenné were restored as part of the Dutch–Malian project Réhabilitation et Conservation de l'Architecture de Djenné, which was devoted to the renovation and maintenance of Djenné's architecture. One of the spin-offs of this large-scale project—in which Boubakar was employed as supervisor of work and materials and liaison officer—was the foundation of GIE DJEBAC: Groupement d'intérêt économique Djenné Barey Construction (in Songhay, *barey* means mason), a company that Boubakar founded together with his friend Gouro Bocoum, who was trained as a technical draftsman. In recent years GIE DJEBAC has carried out various building projects in Djenné and further afield. Business is going well. At the moment the company is in the running for the contract to build Djenné's new museum. Tenders must be submitted very soon.

Because Boubakar will be coming with us tomorrow to Bamako, where he must get visas for himself and his team of masons for their trip to the Netherlands, he and Gouro have been very busy these last few days, getting everything ready for their next project. I've hardly seen him all day.

Even now—Aminata has just brought our special "farewell meal" up to the roof—he's nowhere to be seen. Nan and I are sitting in front of a small portable television; downstairs there's a much larger TV, hooked up to a satellite dish. Elhadji is lying next to us on a mat. We're watching a music program on the Malian channel.

Before she goes back downstairs, Aminata urges us to eat, but just as Nan and I are heaping our plates with *kata* (a local pasta dish), Yousouf shows up. We cover our plates and greet the marabout. As usual, Yousouf does not shake hands with Nan, but raises both hands in a friendly gesture of greeting. He takes a seat across from us, and I tell him we're leaving for Bamako tomorrow. He knows, he says, because he ran into Boubakar as he was leaving the mosque. He's come to say goodbye and wish us a safe journey. When I ask Yousouf how his wife and children are, he tells me that his wife just had a baby last Monday. Tired, and with my mind on our impending departure, I make the mistake I was always afraid I'd make: I offer condolences instead of congratulations. I say "*Yer Koy ma hinje ga,*" a standard expression of condolence meaning "May God forgive him," instead of "*Yer Koy ma hunandi ga*" ("May God let him live"), which is the usual wish for a newborn baby. Yousouf is shocked, and asks if I've understood correctly. I immediately realize what I've done. Embarrassed, I apologize and ask whether it's a boy or a girl. It's a boy. "May God let him live!" I exclaim.

Yousouf tells us to go on eating. I invite him to join us, but he declines. Kata doesn't agree with his stomach, he says. As we eat, Yousouf stares at the television. The interviewer on the young people's program is having a long and extremely dull conversation in French with a theater producer. Yousouf doesn't understand a word of it. Now and then we exchange a desultory sentence. I ask him if he also has a TV, and he says he hasn't had an opportunity to buy one yet.

Boubakar finally arrives and greets Yousouf, and the two strike up a conversation. When Nan and I finish eating, Yousouf makes a move to leave. He stands up, says goodbye to Nan, and wishes her a safe trip. Boubakar and I accompany Yousouf downstairs. In the dark street in front of Boubakar's house, Yousouf sticks out his hand, but when I try to shake it, he remains standing with his hand outstretched, palm upward. He wants to recite gaara. Boubakar and I stretch out our right arms and hold our hands near Yousouf's while he recites the blessings in a soft voice. All of a sudden Ali Farka's guitar chords burst onto the scene: Boubakar's phone is ringing in his pocket. I hear Boubakar murmuring something in Bamana, "*An-ka-taa*" (here best translated as "Hurry up!"). I'm not sure if he's addressing Yousouf or his cell phone, but I do notice how agitated he becomes. After a few bars of music, the ring tone stops. Unperturbed, Yousouf goes on with his blessings. When he says in a normal voice "Al Fatiha," we all three hold both hands in front of us, palms upward, and murmur the first sura of the Qur'an. Then Yousouf recites a final blessing and blows on our palms to pass on the baraka. We wipe our hands over our faces.

There are no lingering farewells. Yousouf turns and disappears into the darkness. Boubakar hurries inside. As I follow him up the stairs, I hear him say, "That's good." I assume he's talking to me, but just as I'm about to agree that the marabout's blessings were indeed a good thing, I notice that he's talking into his phone.

Glossary

With the exception of a few Arabic words, the terms listed below conform to the variant of Songhay spoken in Djenné: *Djenné chiini*. A number of these are loan words from the Arabic. The etymology of some of these terms is discussed in the text. My spelling of Songhay is based on Jeffrey Heath's *Dictionnaire Songhay-Anglais-Français, tome II—Djenné chiini* (L'Harmattan, Paris, 1998).

alfaa: marabout

alhidjaba: protective amulet

aliifu-aliifu: first stage of elementary Qur'anic education

almudu (Arabic: *mawlid*): celebration of the birthday of the Prophet Muhammad (twelfth *Rabi' al-awwal,* the third month in the Islamic calendar). In Djenné it is Muhammad's name day (eighteenth *Rabi' al-awwal*) that is the cause of particular celebration.

baraka (Arabic) (Songhay: *albarka*): blessing, grace, beneficent force

bayaanu: clarity, lucidity; in the sense of "open," as opposed to secret (*sirri*)

buruj (Arabic): sign of the zodiac

chow-koray: third stage of elementary Qur'anic education

dabari: harmful magic

djinn (Arabic) (Songhay: *jinni*): spirits

duʿâ' (Arabic): blessing, petitionary prayer, invocation of God; to bless

fiqh (Arabic): Islamic jurisprudence

fita: sheet or page; fifth and last stage of elementary Qur'anic education

gaara: blessing, petitionary prayer, invocation of God; to bless

garibu: beggar-pupil; Qur'anic student who earns his living by begging

hafiz (Arabic): someone who has learned the entire Qur'an by heart

jingar: prayer; to pray, in the sense of performing one of the five daily ritual prayers

jiiri alkabaar: new year's tidings, predictions of the nature of a certain year read aloud at the beginning of the Islamic year

jiiri-fita: "year-sheets," manuscript containing the new year's tidings

khairun: fourth stage of elementary Qur'anic education; the stage at which instruction in writing begins

madrasah (Arabic): school (within the modernized Islamic educational system)

majlisu: school for advanced Qur'anic education, also called *kitaabu-tirahuu* (book school)

malaika (Arabic): angel

nesi: liquid amulet, amulet water; water in which an amulet text has been dissolved

nesi-kusu: jar holding the water in which pupils at Qur'anic schools wash off their writing boards

salât (Arabic): prayer; to pray, in the sense of performing one of the five daily ritual prayers

saraa (Arabic: *sadaqa*): alms, donation

sirri: secret, as opposed to open or public (*bayaanu*); secret knowledge

tafsîr (Arabic): Qur'anic exegesis

talibé: religious student; in Djenné in particular, a student at the advanced level of Islamic education

tasbiya: prayer beads

timiti-timiti: second stage of elementary Qur'anic education

tira: an amulet that can be worn on the body or hung in the house

tirahuu: elementary Qur'anic school

turaabu: method of divination based on Arabic geomancy

waaju (Arabic: *wa'z*): sermon

Yer Koy naarey: "entreating God" (cf. gaara)

Yer Koy: God (literally "Our Lord")

Bibliography

Ba, A. H., and J. Daget
1955　L'Empire peul du Macina I (1818–1853). Bamako: Institut Français D'Afrique Noire, Centre du Soudan.

Bastien, C.
1988　Folies, mythes et magies d'Afrique noire. Paris: L'Harmattan.

Bedaux, R., D. Diaby, and P. Maas, eds.
2003　L'architecture de Djenné (Mali). La pérennité d'un Patrimoine Mondial. Leiden: Rijksmuseum voor Volkenkunde.

Bedaux, R., and J. van der Waals, eds.
1994　Djenné, une ville millenaire au Mali. Leiden: Rijksmuseum voor Volkenkunde.

Bourgeois, J.-L.
1987　The History of the Great Mosques of Djenné. African Arts XX(3):54–62, 90–92.

Bourgeois, J.-L., and C. Pelos
1989　Spectacular Vernacular: The Adobe Tradition. New York: Aperture Foundation Inc.

Bravmann, R. A.
1983　African Islam. Washington: Smithsonian Institution Press.

Brenner, L.
1985a　The "Esoteric Sciences" in West African Islam. *In* African Healing Strategies. B. M. Du Toit and I. Abdalla, eds. Pp. 20–27. Buffalo, NY: Trado-Medic Books.

1985b　Reflexions sur le savoir islamique en Afrique de l'Ouest. Bourdeaux: Centre d'Etude d'Afrique Noire, Université de Bordeaux I.

2001　Controlling Knowledge: Religion, Power and Schooling in a West African Muslim Society. Bloomington & Indianapolis: Indiana University Press.

Brunet-Jailly, J., ed.
1999   Djenné. D'hier à demain. Bamako: Editions Donniya.

Buitelaar, M.
1993   Fasting and Feasting in Morocco: Women's Participation in Ramadan. Oxford: Berg Publishers.

Buitelaar, M., and H. Motzki, eds.
1993   De Koran: Ontstaan, interpretaties en praktijk. Muiderberg: Coutinho.

Caillié, R.
1985[1830]   Journal d'un voyage à Tombouctou et à Jenne. 2 tomes. Paris: Editions La Découverte.

Cissé, S.
1992   L'Enseignement Islamique en Afrique Noire. Paris: L'Harmattan.

Clarke, P. B.
1982   West Africa and Islam. A Study of Religious Development from the 8th to the 20th Century. London: Edward Arnold.

Cuoq, J. H.
1984   Histoire de l'Islamisation de l'Afrique de l'Ouest. Des origines à la fin du xvie siècle. Paris: Librairie Orientaliste Paul Geuthner SA.

Danner, V.
1988   The Islamic Tradition, an Introduction. New York: Amity House.

Davidson, B.
1972   A History of West Africa, 1000–1800. London: Longman.

Denffer, D. von
1976   Baraka as basic concept of Muslim popular belief. Islamic Studies 15(3):167–186.

Doutté, E.
1909   Magie et Religion dans l'Afrique du Nord. Alger: Adolphe Jordan.

Dubois, F.
1969[1897]   Timbuctoo the Mysterious. D. White, trans. New York: Negro Universities Press.

Eickelman, D. F.
1982   The Study of Islam in Local Contexts. Contributions to Asian Studies 17:1–16.

El-Tom, A. O.
1983   Religious Men and Literacy in Berti Society. Ph.D. dissertation, University of St. Andrews.

1985   Drinking the Koran: The Meaning of Koranic Verses in Berti Erasure. Africa 55(4):414–431.

1987   Berti Qur'anic Amulets. Journal of Religion in Africa XVII(3):224–244.

Es-Sa'di, Abderrahman ben Abdallah ben ʿImrân ben ʿAmir
1964[1913–1914]   Tarikh Es-Soudan. O. Houdas, trans. Paris: Maisonneuve.

Fisher, H. J.
1973   Hassebu: Islamic Healing in Black Africa. *In* Northern Africa: Islam and Modernization. M. Brett, ed. Pp. 23–47. London: Frank Cass.

Gallais, J.
1984   Hommes du Sahel, espaces-temps et pouvoirs, le Delta intérieur du Niger 1960–1980. Paris: Flammarion.

Gardet, L.
1965   Du^{c}â'. Encyclopaedia of Islam. New edition. Vol. II. Pp. 617–618. Leiden: E.J. Brill.

Gardi, B., P. Maas, and G. Mommersteeg
1995   Djenné il y a cent ans. Amsterdam: Institut Royal des Tropiques.

Gatti, R.-C.
1999   Le scuole coraniche di Djenné: Retaggi culturali-censimento-problemi-prospettive, tesi di laurea, Università degli Studi di Genova.

2000   Les écoles coraniques de Djenné: Problèmes et perspectives. Djenné Patrimoine Informations 9:19–36.

Graham, W. A.
1987   Beyond the Written Word. Oral Aspects of Scripture in the History of Religion. Cambridge: Cambridge University Press.

Hamès, C.
1987   *Taktub* ou la magie de l'écriture islamique. Textes soninké à usage magique. Arabica XXXIV:305–325.

1997   Le Coran talismanique, de l'Arabie des origines à l'Afrique occidentale contemporaine. *In* Religion et pratiques de puissance. A. Surgy, ed. Pp. 129–160. Paris: L'Harmattan.

2001   L'usage talismanique du Coran. Revue de l'histoire des religions 218(1):83–95.

Hamès, C., ed.
2007   Coran et talismans. Textes et pratiques en milieu musulman. Paris: Karthala.

Harrison, C.
1988   France and Islam in West Africa, 1860–1960. Cambridge: Cambridge University Press.

Holy, L.
1991   Religion and Custom in a Muslim Society: The Berti of Sudan. Cambridge: Cambridge University Press.

Ibn Khaldun, Abd al-Rahman b. Muhammad
1967   The Muqaddimah: An Introduction to History. F. Rosenthal, trans. N. J. Dawood, abridged and ed. London: Routledge & Kegan Paul.

Jansen, W., ed.
1985   Lokale Islam. Muiderberg: Coutinho.

Kriss, R., and H. Kriss-Heinrich
1962   Volksglaube im Bereich des Islam (Band II: Amulette, Zauberformeln und Beschwörungen). Wiesbaden: Otto Harrassowitz.

Lange, K.
2001   Djénné. West Africa's Eternal City. National Geographic, June 2001:100–117.

Launay, R.
1992   Beyond the Stream. Islam and Society in a West African Town. Berkeley: University of California Press.

La Violette, A.
1987   An Archeological Ethnography of Blacksmiths, Potters and Masons in Jenne, Mali. Ph.D. dissertation, Washington University, Saint Louis.

1995   Women Craft Specialists in Jenne. The Manipulation of Mande Social Categories. *In* Status and Identity in West Africa. D. Conrad and B. Frank, eds. Pp. 170–181. Bloomington & Indianapolis: Indiana University Press.

Maas, P.
1991   Djenné: Living Tradition. Aramco World 41(6):18–29.

Maas, P., and G. Mommersteeg
1989   De Moskee van Djenné, morfologie en onderhoud van een Afrikaans monument. Bulletin KNOB 6:24–30.

1992   Djenné: Chef d'oeuvre architectural. Amsterdam: Institut Royal des Tropiques/KIT.

1993   L'architecture dite soudanaise: Le modèle de Djenné. *In* Vallées du Niger. J. Devisse, ed. Pp. 478–492. Paris: Musée National des Arts D'Afrique et D'Océanie.

Marchand, T.
2009   The Masons of Djenné. Bloomington & Indianapolis: Indiana University Press.

Maupoil, B.
1943   Contribution à l'étude de l'origine musulman de la géomancie dans le Bas-Dahomey. Journal de la Société des Africanistes 13(6):1–94.

McIntosh, S., and R. McIntosh
1980   Prehistoric Investigations at Jenne, Mali (B.A.R. International Series 89, Cambridge Monographs in African Archaeology 2), I-II. Oxford: B.A.R.

1982   Finding West Africa's Oldest City. National Geographic, September 1982:396–418.

Mommersteeg, G.
1988   "He Has Smitten Her to the Heart with Love." The Fabrication of an Islamic Love-Amulet in West Africa. Anthropos 83(4/6):501–510.

1989   Djenné vraagt om regen. Islamitische regenrituelen in een stad in de Sahel. Etnofoor 2(1):71–83.

1990   Allah's Words as Amulet. Etnofoor 3(1):63–76.

1991a   L'Education coranique au Mali: Le pouvoir des mots sacrés. *In* L'Enseignement Islamique au Mali. B. Sanankoua and L. Brenner, eds. Pp. 45–61. Bamako: Editions Jamana.

1991b   Learning the Word of God. Aramco World 42(5):2–10.

1994   Marabouts à Djenné; enseignement coranique, invocations et amulettes. *In* Djenné; une ville millénaire au Mali. R. Bedaux and D. v.d. Waals, eds. Pp. 64–75. Leiden: Rijksmuseum voor Volkenkunde.

1995   *Siri*, het geheim van de marabout: Enkele etnografische aantekeningen over religieuze kennis in Mali. Medische Antropologie 7(1):85–100.

1996   Het domein van de marabout. Koranleraren en magisch-religieuze specialisten in Djenné (Mali). Ph.D. dissertation, Utrecht University.

1999   Qur'anic Teachers and Magico-Religious Specialists in Djenné. Newsletter International Institute for the Study of Islam in the Modern World (ISIM) 3:30.

2003   Au-déla du banco. Quelques remarques sur les secrets des maçons de Djenné. *In* L'Architecture de Djenné. Pérennité d'un Patrimoine Mondial. R. Bedaux, B. Diaby, and P. Maas, eds. Pp. 24–27. Leiden: Rijksmuseum voor Volkenkunde.

2004   Djenné demande de la pluie. Prières et rituels pour obtenir la pluie dans une ville sahélienne. Djenné Patrimoine Informations 16:11–14.

2005a   Bénédictions et amulettes. Quelques remarques sur la connaissance des marabouts à Djenné. Djenné Patrimoine Informations 18:9–12.

2005b   "Seul Dieu connaît l'avenir." Quelques notes ethnographiques sur la divination en milieu musulman à Djenné (Mali). Mande Studies 7:99–117.

Monteil, C.
1903   Monographie de Djénné, cercle et ville. Tulle: Jean Mazeyrie.
1971[1932]   Une cité soudanaise: Djénné. Métropole du Delta Central du Niger. Paris: Edition Anthropos.

Monteil, V.
1980[1964]   L'Islam noir, une réligion à la conquête de l'Afrique. Paris: Editions de Seuil.

Moreau, R. L.
1982   Africains Musulmans. Paris: Présence Africaine.

Mulder, D. C.
1983   The ritual of the recitation of the Qur'an. Nederlands Theologisch Tijdschrift 37(3):247–252.

Olivier, E.
2004   La petite musique de la ville. Musique et construction de la citadinité à Djenné (Mali). Journal des Africanistes 74(1/2):97–123.

Owusu-Ansah, D.
1991   Islamic Talismanic Tradition in Nineteenth-Century Asante. Lewiston: The Edwin Mellen Press.

Padwick, C. E.
1969[1961]   Muslim Devotions. A Study of Prayer-Manuals in Common Use. London: S.P.C.K.

Park, M.
1983[1799]   Travels into the Interior of Africa. London: Eland.

Prussin, L.
1986   Hatumere: Islamic Design in West Africa. Berkeley: University of California Press.

Sanankoua, B., and L. Brenner, eds.
1991   L'Enseignement Islamique au Mali. Bamako: Editions Jamana.

Santerre, R.
1973   Pédagogie musulmane d'Afrique noire. Montréal: Les Presses de l'Université de Montréal.

Soares, B.
2005   Islam and the Prayer Economy. History and Authority in a Malian Town. Edinburgh: Edinburgh University Press.

Tamari, T.
2002   Islamic Higher Education in West Africa: Some Examples from Mali. *In* Islam in Africa (Yearbook of the Sociology of Islam 4). T. Bierschenk and G. Stauth, eds. Pp. 91–128. Münster: Lit Verlag.

Trimingham, J. S.
1959   Islam in West Africa. Oxford: University Press.

Waardenburg, J., ed.
1987   Islam: Norm, ideaal en werkelijkheid. Weesp: Het Wereldvenster.

Wessels, A.
1986   De Koran Verstaan. Kampen: Uitgeversmaatschappij J.H. Kok.

Yattara, A. M., and B. Salvaing
2000   Almamy. Une jeunesse sur les rives du fleuve Niger. Brinon-sur-Sauldre: Editions Grandvaux.

2003   Almamy. L'âge d'homme d'un lettré malien. Brinon-sur-Sauldre: Editions Grandvaux.

Yousif, A. W. A.
1985   Islam and Adult Education. The International Encyclopedia of Education. Vol. 5:2711–2714. Oxford: Pergamon Press.